South African Anthropology in Conversation
An Intergenerational Interview on the History and Future of Social Anthropology in South Africa

Jessica L. Dickson
in conversation with
Andrew D. Spiegel

T0319184

Langaa Research & Publishing CIG
Mankon, Bamenda

Publisher:
Langaa RPCIG
Langaa Research & Publishing Common Initiative Group
P.O. Box 902 Mankon
Bamenda
North West Region
Cameroon
Langaagrp@gmail.com
www.langaa-rpcig.net

Distributed in and outside N. America by African Books Collective
orders@africanbookscollective.com
www.africanbookcollective.com

ISBN: 9956-792-39-X

DISCLAIMER
All views expressed in this publication are those of the author and do not necessarily reflect the views of Langaa RPCIG.

About the Book

In the 1980s, the University of Cape Town's social anthropology department was predominantly oriented by a neo-Marxist approach that focused on an 'exposé' style of critical scholarship. The enemy was the apartheid state, the ethical imperative was clear and a combative metaphor for doing research that revealed the effects of state oppression motivated the department. Andrew David Spiegel, known affectionately as 'Mugsy' by his students, has been a central, if understated, figure of the discipline in South Africa.

In a series of interviews between the senior professor and his student, Mugsy offers a unique perspective from the centre of anthropology's recent history in South Africa, yet from the insightful peripheries of its more commonly known narrative. His story recounts the experiences of one academic who was there; who helped frame the theoretical charge of a generation of students looking for new ways to counter apartheid from 'inside' and, notably, from a position of privilege that apartheid had helped to ensure.

However, these intergenerational conversations are as much about the present and the future of South African anthropology as they are about its past. Faced with the persistent uncertainties of institutional transformation and unresolved questions regarding the discipline's relevance to independent Africans, a new generation searches for new approaches to engage the complexities of neoliberalism and postcolonial subjectivity. And yet, if recent events like Marikana suggest the return of apartheid-era disciplines, then Mugsy's experience holds considerable value to South African anthropology well beyond its archive.

About Jessica L. Dickson

Jessica Dickson is a doctoral student in African Studies at Harvard University. Her interests include South African anthropology, postcolonial subjectivity, visual culture and media, African futurism and science fiction studies, with a current research focus on the South African film industry. These interests, and the conversations recorded in this book, emerged while conducting fieldwork on 'township tourism' in Cape Town in 2010. She received a master's of social science from the University of Cape Town in 2011 and completed her BA in anthropology in her hometown at the University of Illinois Urbana-Champaign in 2008. She continues to divide her time between friends, family, and research in South Africa, Illinois, and Boston.

Praise for this Book

"This frank and gripping first auto-ethnographic and contextual history of anthropology in South Africa focuses on the decades of struggle and transition since 1970. Mugsy Spiegel speaks from his heart with Jessica Dickson about his socially engaged working life in beautiful, reflexive, conversations. These are testimony to the impact of national politics on academia, Spiegel's pioneering exposé ethnography, his activism through pedagogy and the rifts between theoretical paradigms. The narratives underline the continuing value of political economic analysis based on critical ethnography, in combination with a deep humanism, as embodied in Spiegel's journey that was central to the shaping of a socially relevant anthropology at UCT and nationally."
Kees van der Waal, Professor of Social Anthropology at Stellenbosch University, South Africa.

"Following in the imperative anthropological tradition of auto-critique, 'Mugsy' Spiegel's personal recollections provide meat to the skeleton of previous historical accounts of South African anthropology grappling with its reputation as apartheid's handmaiden. For the younger generation of anthropologists the book provides interesting backstage insights; for those of us who were there, it is an engrossing tour down memory lane."
Dr Emile Boonzaier Boonzaier, co-editor, South African Keywords: The uses and abuses of political concepts (1988)

"In 1994 'Mugsy' Spiegel asked fellow anthropologists 'what do we do now?' For him it has been more of the same. Tireless writing and research on the problems of South Africa and, what this inspirational volume shows, making them known to the future of world anthropology"
Michael Rowlands, Emeritus Professor of Anthropology and Material Culture, University College London, UK.

Table of Contents

Table of Contents

iv

Acknowledgements

Firstly, I would like to thank Francis Nyamnjoh for his persistent enthusiasm and encouragement towards the completion of this publication. Thanks are also owed to Jean and John Comaroff for their feedback and insightful perspective on social anthropology and South African history. Andrew Bank, Fiona Ross, and Emile Boonzaier also gave thoughtful and helpful feedback on earlier drafts of the introduction chapter, for which I am very grateful. Thank you, also, to the staff at Cape Times, DALRO, and the National Library of South Africa for their assistance in locating and securing permissions for many of the images used here. Additionally, revisiting these interviews three years later has increased my appreciation for the professors and lecturers under whom I had the privilege to study during my time as a Master's student at the University of Cape Town. I feel especially indebted to Helen Macdonald, Fiona Ross, Francis Nyamnjoh, Susan Levine and Patti Henderson for their intellectual guidance and inspiration, as well as their honesty about the quandaries and anxieties of conducting research and producing knowledge. Finally, I am hugely grateful to Andrew 'Mugsy' Spiegel for his participation in this project: for sharing his stories, opinions, and perspective with me and for granting me his time and patience during our conversations recorded here and those thereafter.

Conversation Starters

The impetus for the set of interviews given here came from conversations between Andrew 'Mugsy' Spiegel and myself, and a car full of my peers, on a fourteen-hour drive from Cape Town to the 2010 Anthropology Southern Africa conference at the University of Fort Hare. Searching for conversation topics from the front seat, next to the most senior professor of my department, I fell back on questions that had first led me, as a young Midwest-American college student, to move to South Africa to pursue a degree. Here, I realised, was someone who had been around during the events I had read about with rapt attention and romanticism as a younger student. "What was the reaction at UCT when Steve Biko was murdered? What was it like to be doing field research in Soweto in '76? What was it like to be a white university student during apartheid? What was it like when they announced the release of Mandela?" While I had been nervous that my questions would come off as naïve to both my professor and my South African classmates, they seemed to kick-start a conversation about doing anthropology under apartheid and after, one that would last all the way to East London.

The production of this book is intended to coincide with Spiegel's retirement from the University of Cape Town at the end of 2014. The historical outline given in the introductory chapter is admittedly UCT-centric, which is partly a reflection of my own bias as a recent UCT student and my current inability to conduct the amount of historical research needed to offer broader institutional histories of South African universities. It is also because UCT's history, for the last forty-two years, has also been Andrew Spiegel's, and his contributions to anthropology are additionally his contributions to the university.

In truth, a more experienced student with a firmer grasp of South African history would have been better suited for the job of turning these conversations into interviews. My biases, assumptions, and general ignorance about many topics surely come through to the careful reader in the following pages, but perhaps Spiegel's need to repeatedly set me straight kept him talking. Also, I hope, I may have asked questions that my colleagues would have thought too obvious to ask. In this regard, Francis Nyamnjoh has enthusiastically encouraged this project as the first of many intergenerational—and in my case, international—conversations between anthropologists. I have come to think of these interviews as a kind of artifact of the social reproduction of the discipline of anthropology; repetition with a difference, across time and borders.

An Introduction to Intergenerational Conversations with a Combative Anthropologist

Jessica Dickson

Jess: Did much argument for activism come up in the '80s? Over whether anthropologists should be activists in the struggle?

Mugsy: Of course. Yeah it did. I mean, we saw ourselves as activists— in 1990, the second of February, when de Klerk made his speech to say that he was going to release Nelson Mandela, unban the ANC and the PAC and everything else, and slowly release all the political prisoners and move towards something else, a new arrangement .... Martin West—in the Head of Department's office—and John Sharp, Emile Boonzaier, and I sat there listening to the radio, to hear the speech. At the end of it we looked at each other and said, "What are we gonna do now?"

Because our whole raison d'être had gone. Everything we were doing ... I mean from 1973 or so, when I first started doing stuff, was driven by a concern to show-up what the apartheid state was doing. To try and provide the evidence, expose their stuff. And we said, "Now what?" And we still haven't quite found out. It was easy—it was much easier to be able to identify the enemy [before then]. It was easy. Van der Wateren was the fellow from Potchefstroom that I went for at the [1979] conference. He represented it. The state represented it. They were there, you could see them, they were people, it wasn't neoliberal principles as we have now to target. It wasn't 'The Washington Consensus'. It wasn't things like that. It was a small, narrow-minded government, and a bunch of narrow-minded anthropologists and others who supported them. It was much easier to know who your enemy was. Now it's this diffuse idea. ... Um ... So, yeah, that was what drove us ... which didn't mean we were necessarily there on the streets. (pers comm. 7 April, 2011)

The 1980s of South African anthropology at English-medium universities, particularly at the University of Cape Town (UCT) and the University of Witwatersrand (Wits), was predominantly oriented by a neo-Marxist approach that focused on an 'exposé' style of anthropology. The enemy was the state, the political and ethical imperatives were clear and a combative metaphor for doing research that revealed the effects of state oppression motivated the departments. Andrew David Spiegel, known affectionately as 'Mugsy' by his friends, colleagues, and students, was a central, if sometimes understated, figure of South African social anthropology during this politically tumultuous period.

Having first registered as a student at UCT in 1972, holding a position in the department until the present day, and taking on additional administrative roles in recent years, Spiegel has a unique historical perspective on the university and on anthropology in South Africa. He progressed as a student in the '70s, following the passing of the Bantu Homelands Citizenship Act that would dramatically intensify the dispossessions, resettlements, and labour migrations in rural South Africa, and would become the focus of his early career. He was conducting fieldwork in Soweto as part of Philip Mayer's study on migrant labour in 1976 at the time of the Soweto Uprising and a year later, while at Rhodes University, he saw the response to the murder of Steve Biko when he attended the funeral in King Williams Town's Ginsberg 'Location'.

In the '80s, he and John Sharp rigorously invested in the neo-Marxist paradigm that would allow for the framing of apartheid's effects in South Africa within the global context of capitalist labour exploitation. Colin Murray, whose visa exemption had been withdrawn by the government in response to his work on migrant labour and forced resettlements, was also an important influence on and interlocutor for Spiegel. Murray managed intermittent visits by sneaking across the border from Lesotho to collaborate in these subversive conversations at UCT (Murray-Pepper 2013). Spiegel, Murray, Sharp, and others not only elaborated a theoretical approach that directly attacked the apartheid state and contradicted the *volkekunde*—or 'ethnos theory'—anthropology practised at Afrikaans-medium universities at the time (Sharp 1981), but also trained students in these intellectually combative tactics, creating what Hammond-Tooke called a formidable presence at UCT. He explains:

> The cogency of their arguments, and their undoubted deep concern for the plight of the poor and oppressed, attracted a large following of the more politically aware and thoughtful students. Seminars, in which staff and students from other departments participated, were lively, and shoddy thinking was ruthlessly exposed. (Hammond-Tooke 1997: 176)

The interviews presented here recount Andrew 'Mugsy' Spiegel's personal history as he came to anthropology, including how he developed his theoretical leanings and his political consciousness. This book is therefore intended neither as a festschrift, nor comprehensive memoir of Spiegel's career in anthropology or his life thus far. Rather, this project began as a conversation between a senior professor and his student about his own experiences in anthropology under and after apartheid. As these conversations continued, they came to address less Spiegel's contribution to the discipline through his publications and theoretical innovations than the experiences that provoked his particular questions about sociality; what lead him to his particular field sites; what challenged him to think theoretically and engage combatively with the critical tools he still feels anthropology provides him; and what other anthropologists, through their influence, made such engagements possible?

Admittedly, I pushed Spiegel to talk at greater length about experiences that he sees as leading to his own conscientizing, and some that he insists had no influence on his academic career. Nonetheless, a person's experiences inevitably shape his or her ethics and scholarship. Included, therefore, are Spiegel's stories about his time in the South African military training-camps of the '60s—where he listened via radio to the first moon landing—and his subsequent and successful tactics to avoid military service thereafter. Before 'finding anthropology', as it were, Spiegel studied the physical sciences at Wits where he failed his second-year courses and subsequently dropped out of university. Between 1969 and 1971, Spiegel spent time on a Kibbutz in Israel, participated in a voluntary service-camp in Lesotho that would profoundly influence his future research interests, and transferred to UCT to study economic history, anthropology and Sesotho. Once, thrown unwittingly into the middle of a standoff between an alleged carjacker and a group of armed vigilantes, Spiegel stood his ground as a would-be witness and successfully stalled mob justice in a Johannesburg industrial district. He once found himself detained by the then Transkei police and was subsequently accosted by South African security police while conducting research in the Transkei's Matatiele District, becoming entangled in local jealousies and being accused—by the then South African ambassador to the Transkei, Marais Steyn—of "pissing on a pig". Earlier, as a young student in August 1968, his photo made the papers—stripped, beaten, and shaved by University of Pretoria students, along with four of his peers at Wits—for publicly protesting UCT's retraction of anthropologist Archie Mafeje's appointment.

These stories are entwined with Spiegel's account of departmental histories across South Africa in the '60s, '70s and '80s, about which he has published and on which he has spent considerable time reflecting.[1] In doing so he has attempted, like other South African anthropologists who remained 'inside' during the apartheid years (Hammond-Tooke 1997; Kuper 1998; Bank and Bank 2013), to explain anthropology's particular history under state oppression; to vindicate and, to some extent—given pressures he experienced while he was Head of Department—to salvage social anthropology and the neo-Marxist paradigms that came to dominate English-medium universities in the latter years of the regime. Following John Sharp's lead, he also sought to differentiate these interventions from the clearer-cut complicity of the *volkekunde* anthropologists that would directly serve, and help to shape, the ideologies of apartheid's social architecture (Sharp 1981; Hammond-Tooke 1997).

---

[1] See Spiegel 1989, 1997, 2005, 2007; Spiegel and McAllister 1991; Gordon and Spiegel 1993.

While government constraints made fieldwork during this period incredibly difficult, Spiegel and other social anthropologists working within the country continued to publish critical research under conditions of state emergency.[2] Participant-observation under apartheid included police surveillance, the persistent scrutiny of people's research and, perhaps most importantly, the questions brought to the fore about the ethics of conducting research at all, given the state of things. David Webster saw this clearly, devoted himself to activism, and paid the ultimate price. Whether or not scholarship at the time was framed in opposition to the state, the fear remained that any knowledge gathered under the banner of research could always be turned into an instrument of oppressive knowledge/power. And at what point might a person's interlocutors be put at risk by simply asking them questions? Conversely, what were the ethics of *not* conducting research; of neglecting the critical tools wielded by social theory to expose and deconstruct the agenda of a repressive state?

And, looking forward, this returns us to the question Spiegel rhetorically poses above: When a department has framed its disciplinary impetus around 'writing against' something—in this case, the apartheid state—despite, and indeed *because of*, its persistent hazards, what is to be done when that something seems to have resolved itself? "Seems to" being the operative phrase here, of course. A further question that troubled these anthropologists in the '90s was: when all these constraints had gone away, why was anthropology in South Africa not flourishing in the ways they had so deeply hoped and expected (Gordon and Spiegel 1993: 84-85)? Moreover, is this trend changing at present, and if so, what exactly *has* changed after two decades of democratic transition? Several suggestions are given below and in my recorded conversations with Spiegel reproduced here.

The excerpts from Spiegel's narrative are therefore intended as an entry point into the history of South African anthropology, though not at its beginning. It constitutes a story from the

---

2 See Mafeje 1981; McAllister 1986; Murray 1981, 1983, 1987; Reynolds 1989; Sharp 1987; Sharp and Spiegel 1985; Spiegel 1986, 1989; Webster 1988 and many others.

perspective of one academic who was there, who helped frame the mission and the theoretical charge of a generation of students looking for a new way to counter apartheid from inside its borders, under its constraints, and, notably, from a position of privilege that apartheid had helped to ensure—an admittedly awkward position from which to fight a system of power. And yet, as Spiegel explains, he does not expect to be particularly remembered for his role. Teaching, he often suggests, has been the method of his activism. While his reflections on the past and concerns for the future can at times seem cynical, the high standards he maintains for teaching and supervision, and his continued efforts to foster interconnections between anthropologists across the globe through his work with multiple international anthropological associations betrays a persistent optimism. [3]

A closer and more thorough consideration of Spiegel's work in context and in collaboration with his colleagues, interlocutors, and students—many of whom hold positions of academic authority today—is greatly warranted. While the interviews and the brief historical outline presented here cannot compare to the kind of comprehensive and revelatory life history offered by Bank and Bank (2013), for example, in their recent biography of Monica Wilson, it is my hope that it might contribute to their case "for broadening the criterion by which significance may be judged" (2). From here I offer a brief background of this history, recounted with greater complexity and depth elsewhere by Spiegel, his colleagues, and his predecessors in the discipline.

Anthropology in South Africa: Beginnings and Ruptures

Africanist anthropology, in many ways, still grapples with its alleged role as the 'handmaiden' of colonialism. Though tempered by attention to the ambiguities of colonial history, the assertion still strikes at the core of any anthropologist working in Africa, as the most urgent topics of research still largely concern colonialism's

---

[3] These associations include Anthropology Southern Africa, the Pan African Association of Anthropologists, the International Union of Anthropological and Ethnological Sciences and the World Council of Anthropological Associations.

legacy and its negative effects on the continent and beyond. South African anthropology is uniquely implicated in this critique, however, due to its own disciplinary development alongside the apartheid state. While several celebrated anthropologists left the country in reaction to the regime and went on to establish impressive careers in the United States and Europe—scholars like Max Gluckman, Meyer Fortes, Archie Mafeje, Bernard Magubane, Peter Carstens, Graeme Watson, Adam Kuper, John Blacking, Jean and John Comaroff, and Robert Gordon—several others stayed behind (Hammond-Tooke 1997: 3). Since the early '80s, much has been published by anthropologists, both 'inside' and out of South Africa, delineating how the intellectual labour of those who remained contributed to, or otherwise impacted, the ideological structures of the apartheid state.[4]

In *Imperfect Interpreters* (1997), W. D. Hammond-Tooke offers academic biographies mixed with personal insights on some of the discipline's key actors between 1920 and 1990. In addition to interrogating the actual involvement of these scholars in state policy and practice, he also explores—more optimistically—their contribution to anthropological theory in the wider world. His influential overview has also been criticized, however, for its androcentric focus (Bank and Bank 2013). While mentioned, Hammond-Tooke gives short shrift to the contributions of anthropologists like Winifred Hoernlé, Ellen Hellmann, Monica Wilson, Eileen Krige, and Hilda Kuper and to what Lyn Schumaker (2008) has called "the feminisation of social anthropology" in Africa during the interwar years (in Bank and Bank 2013: 13).[5] What is clear, however, is that different anthropologists related to the state in radically different ways and there has been considerable effort to

---

[4] See West 1979; Sharp 1981; Whisson 1986; Gordon and Spiegel 1993; Scheper-Hughes 1995; Hammond-Tooke 1997; Kuper 1998; Bank and Bank 2013.

[5] The brief historical outline I offer here, and the interviews that follow, do not adequately address the need to revise a male-dominated narrative of the history of anthropology in southern Africa. Bank and Bank's *Inside African Anthropology: Monica Wilson and her Interpreters* (2013) better attends to this redress, as will Andrew Bank's forthcoming study, *Pioneers of the Field: South Africa's Women Anthropologists*.

recover, distinguish, and account for the two streams of anthropological theory that predominated in South African universities in the twentieth century, namely the Afrikaans-based *volkekunde* and the British-born structural-functionalism of South African social anthropology (See Sharp 1981).

While much is owed to earlier ethnographic writing on South Africa by influential travel-writers and missionaries like Henri-Alexander Junod and journalist Solomon T. Plaatje, the beginning of anthropology as a discipline in South Africa is historically located at the University of Cape Town in 1921, with the establishment of the first anthropology department under A.R. Radcliffe-Brown. Although Radcliffe-Brown held his position at UCT for just five years, he is credited with having outlined, during that time, a distinct departure from then-popular diffusionist models of anthropology to a structural-functionalist analysis that would predominate in British social anthropology for several decades. Relying heavily on Durkheimian sociology, Radcliffe-Brown's structural-functionalist paradigm promoted an approach to society as an organic whole rather than discrete groups and was antithetical to what would become the explicit ideology and social architecture of apartheid (Hammond-Tooke 1997: 15-17, 24-31).

Anthropology departments were later established in all the major universities of South Africa, the most influential of which generated a 'Golden Age of South African Ethnography' between the 1930s and 1950s by such notable names as Isaac Schapera, Winifred Hoernlé, Ellen Hellman, Monica Wilson, Hilda Kuper, and Eileen and Jack Krige (Hammond-Tooke 1997: 2). Although the influence of apartheid led to a period of relative isolation of South African anthropology from the intellectual centers of Europe and North America in the '60s and '70s, through renowned scholars like Max Gluckman, Meyer Fortes, Isaac Schapera and those other South African anthropologists who pursued careers abroad, channels of intellectual exchange did continue (3, 107). Approaches beyond structural-functionalism were soon needed, however, and alternative models developed in response to the radical social transformations taking shape under the apartheid state in later decades.

Distinct from the structural-functionalists of South African anthropology's so-called 'Golden Age', Sharp (1981) and Gordon (1988) have most notably given a historical account of the *volkekunde* anthropology practised and proliferated by Afrikaans-medium universities in the country—namely Stellenbosch, Pretoria, Potchefstroom, and the Orange Free State—from the 1920s until the mid-'80s (Hammond-Tooke 1997: 15). The emphasis placed by the *volkekundiges* on primordially distinct cultures constituting ethnic groups contributed immensely to apartheid ideology and many would eventually hold state administrative positions. Prominent among its practitioners was W. W. M. Eiselen, head of the first *volkekunde* department established in 1928 at the University of Stellenbosch, who would go on to head the same department at Pretoria, serve on the Commission of Inquiry into Bantu Education, and become Secretary for Native Affairs under Verwoerd in 1950 (Sharp 1981: 29). Eiselen was then followed at both Stellenbosch and Pretoria by P.J. Coertze, who co-authored the 1943 publication, *The Solution of the Native Problem in South Africa: Suggestions Concerning the Afrikaner Standpoint on Apartheid,* which laid down a comprehensive ideological framework that would be a blueprint for apartheid policy (Hammond-Tooke 1997: 125-6).

Although these *volkekundiges* claimed to draw from both Malinowski and an American approach to cultural anthropology, they demonstrated a strong influence from evolutionism, pre-World War II German Philosophy, and a Christian-National religious mandate of racial superiority. Eiselen's and Coertze's students propagated *volkekunde* alongside an Afrikaner Nationalism across Afrikaans-medium universities and the bureaucratic apparatuses of the apartheid state after its inauguration in 1948 (Sharp 1981: 31; Hammond-Tooke 1997: 124-127, 130). Granted that the distinction between the *volkekundiges* and the early structural-functionalist anthropologists appears stark, at least with regard to their relative contributions to apartheid policy; yet the complex of capillaries that flow between academic theory and political ideology is a more complicated story.

The structural-functionalist focus of a Radcliffe-Brownian social anthropology promoted models of society as integrated wholes with universalist properties. Many of the monographs written by the social anthropologists in the early to mid-twentieth century therefore focused on social entities such as 'the Zulu', 'the Lovedu' etc. as seemingly distinctive societies and treated them as their 'units of analysis'. With titles like *The Social System of the Zulus* (Krige 1936), *The Realm of a Rain-Queen: A Study of the Pattern of Lovedu Society* (Krige and Krige 1943), *The Lineage Principle in Gusii Society* (Mayer 1951), *Communal Rituals of the Nyakyusa* (Wilson 1959), or simply, *Bhaca Society* (Hammond-Took 1962), they appeared to represent the same kind of bounded cultures as did the works of the *volkekundiges*. Many classical structural-functionalist works have thus also been criticized for reifying notions of distinct social boundaries and homogenous groups; to stress equilibrium over change and grand dynamics over individual action.[6]

Yet *volkekundiges* remained committed to such representations and to seeing distinct cultures as each expressing its own primordial distinctiveness. Social anthropologists, however, including Radcliffe-Brown himself, began to understand South African society as a whole to constitute their significant unit of analysis, albeit with social and cultural differences being played out within it. Max Gluckman's famous 'Analysis of a Social Situation in Modern Zululand' (1940) has become recognised for first emphasing the need to include both Africans and Europeans as a single unit for ethnographic research.[7] As Bank and Bank point out, however, Monica Wilson's attention to 'social change' was also integral to shifting ethnographic frameworks (Bank and Bank 2013: 1-2).[8]

---

[6] See Sharp 1980, 1985 and West 1988. See also Rich (1984) for a discussion of the liberal segregationist movements between the 1920s and 1960s, and Lodge's (1985) critique of Rich that the blanket term of 'liberal' often obscures the more complex intellectual history of individuals who fell variously on "a spectrum of liberalism between 'conservative' endorsement and 'radical' criticism of segregationism" (1985: 339).

[7] See Cocks (2001) on 'Max Gluckman and the Critique of Segregation in South African Anthropology'.

[8] See Godfrey and Monica Wilson's *The Analysis of Social Change: Based on Observations in Central Africa* (1945), which Andrew Bank points out was the first study to use the term 'social change' in its title (Bank 2013: 1).

Indeed, South African social anthropologists have in fact been profoundly concerned with change since the induction of the discipline. Monica Hunter (later Wilson)'s *Reaction to Conquest* (1936), as well as the works of Isaac Schapera, Eileen Krige, and Ellen Hellmann, represent attempts to address social change within a structural-functionalist paradigm as early as the 1930s (Hammond-Tooke 1997: 141-3, 152-3).[9] Still, however, the sharp awareness of the distinctive roles of anthropology, in its various and contested forms, in imagining, manifesting, or confronting the structures of apartheid would fuel anxieties around the ethics of an applied or activist anthropology in South Africa well into the '90s.[10]

South African Anthropology: 1970s and 1980s

Adam Kuper (1998) has described the years between 1960 and 1985 as the most tumultuous and painful of apartheid, ushering in "a period of ideological ferment among oppositional intellectuals" (15). English-medium anthropology departments that had shared an uneasy relationship with *volkekunde* anthropologists in the past now expressed their staunch dissent. The black power movement heralded by Robert Sobukwe and Steve Biko energised black opposition and the African National Congress (ANC), operating in exile, became increasingly Marxist in orientation. Meanwhile, Nelson Mandela and much of the African opposition were imprisoned while forced relocations, stricter pass laws and a system of Bantu Education continued (Kuper 1998: 15-16). Under these conditions, liberal traditions in the social sciences were increasingly seen as irrelevant and more radical, 'revisionist' scholarship in history, sociology, and the political sciences began to emerge (Saunders 1988). By the 1980s, anthropologists like Spiegel, Sharp, Murray and David Webster were busy establishing a neo-Marxist critique, within South African anthropology, of the discipline's conservative attention to culture, ethnicity, and difference.

---

[9] Also noteworthy here is Monica Wilson's later study with Archie Mafeje on Langa in 1963.

[10] See Gordon and Spiegel 1993; Scheper-Hughes 1995; Robins and Scheper-Hughes 1996.

This period also saw a shift in the focus of ethnographic research. While *volkekunde* departments remained relevant primarily to the state and practised a form of academic self-isolation characteristic "of the ethnos *laager*" (Hammond-Tooke 1997: 138), social anthropologists in South Africa began to explore, in greater depth than before and increasingly as their primary focus of attention, questions of urbanisation, migrant labour, rural change, and political economy. Philip and Iona Mayer have been widely recognised for their intervention into assumptions of cultural homogeneity and stasis through their work *Townsmen or Tribesmen* (1974). As Spiegel and McAllister wrote:

> Most importantly ... *Townsmen or Tribesmen* showed how people with their varied experience of apartheid and industrial labour found ways to draw upon the situation in which they found themselves. They were able thereby to resist, at least ideologically, the forces that had drawn them into a foreign system and were increasingly turning them into an oppressed and subordinated proletariat. (1991: 2-3)

By the late '70s and '80s this shifting attention to change, contestation, and resistance intensified into a period of more radical critique involving a neo-Marxist analysis and an exposé style of anthropology, of which Spiegel was an integral part.

The enthusiastic uptake of a neo-Marxist paradigm by many South African social anthropologists, along with many departments of sociology and history in the country, coincided with its growing emphasis in metropolitan scholarship and offered a new generation of South African anthropologists a new theoretical means to challenge the state (Gordon and Spiegel 1993: 89). South African Communist Party member, lawyer, activist, and sociologist Harold Wolpe published his seminal 'Capitalism and Cheap Labour Power in South Africa: From Segregation to Apartheid' in 1972 while exiled in England and energised a discourse around apartheid's role as a mode of capitalist accumulation. Wolpe's work was banned in South Africa, along with other emerging critical scholarship of the time that challenged the prevailing liberal view of South Africa's history with a more radical materialism (Saunders 1988). Spiegel recounts how he and his colleagues circulated such illicit material amongst themselves and attempted to understand and apply it to the circumstances they observed around them and in their own research. Other academics living abroad but who visited South Africa, like Colin Murray, also managed to smuggle in such materials and encouraged the conversation (Chapter 3).

This neo-Marxist turn provided Spiegel and his colleagues a way to link the detrimental circumstances of capitalism in apartheid South Africa to the economic structures of the wider world. With works like 'Rural differentiation and the diffusion of migrant labour remittances in Lesotho' (Spiegel 1980), *Families Divided: The Impact of Migrant Labour in Lesotho* (Murray 1981), 'Vulnerability to impoverishment in South African rural areas: the erosion of kinship and neighborhood as social resources' (Sharp and Spiegel 1985), 'Class and rural differentiation in a rural Kwa-Zulu community' (Webster 1988), 'Domestic dynamics and wage labour' (Niehaus 1988), and 'Towards an understanding of tradition: uses of tradition(al) in Apartheid South Africa' (Spiegel 1989), South African social anthropologists used an emphasis on political economy and structural impoverishment to combat state propaganda and to expose its racist rhetoric as a means to ensure economic privilege for minority rule. The University of Cape Town and University of Witwatersrand in particular earned a reputation for producing critical, materialist scholarship on South Africa during the '80s.

One of the most influential works to come out of South African anthropology during the last few years of the apartheid regime's hold was the 1988 publication, *South African Keywords: The Uses and Abuses of Political Concepts*. '*Keywords*' represented the consolidation of the critical turn then being developed, and it was grounded in the ethnographic studies of leading local scholars at the time. Edited by Emile Boonzaier and John Sharp, its contributors sought to deconstruct notions of 'culture', 'race', 'tribe', 'community', and 'nation-state', with a co-authored chapter on 'tradition' by

Boonzaier and Spiegel.[11] These contentious terms, they argued, had been strategically deployed and manipulated by the apartheid state and the *volkekundiges* to legitimise a regime of racial exclusion. *'Keywords'* was read widely across disciplines and outside of academia and its deconstructivist project was reflected in the classroom.

Transitions and Traditions: the 1990s

Two years after the publication of *'Keywords'* (1988), the apartheid government began its institutional deconstruction, having lost its ideological stronghold both inside the country and in the eyes of international and economic stakeholders. Landmarked by Spiegel as the moment he and his colleagues at UCT stood around the radio in the office of Martin West, the then Head of Department, the department and the discipline of anthropology began a period of uncertain transition along with the rest of the country. As Spiegel explains above,[12] since the mid-twentieth century, the *raison d'être* of the UCT anthropology department had been to confront apartheid by exposing the abuses and myths put forward by those in power and to explore the interface between people and an oppressive state; between coloniser and colonized. By the mid-'90s, police interference in and surveillance of academic research, along with the imposition of bureaucratic obstacles, had largely ceased. Student enrollment was high, though still predominantly white. And yet, the direction and relevance of the discipline in South Africa had become uncertain. As violent conflict between political factions increased during the interim period of apartheid's fall in 1990 and the first democratic election in 1994, it became increasingly unclear where to aim the discipline's finely-honed and combative critique; the same applied to the location of the most ethical space of academic engagement and applied intervention (Gordon and Spiegel 1993; Robins 1996; Spiegel 1997).

---

[11] Although published prior to it, the chapter built on Spiegel's (1989) 'Towards an understanding of tradition: uses of tradition(al) in Apartheid South Africa'.

[12] Also see Gordon and Spiegel 1993:100.

The solutions offered for the dilemmas posed by transition, as Spiegel also indicates, have yet to prove wholly satisfactory.

As the '90s progressed, Marxist paradigms of broad systems and dependency theories began to show their shortcomings under the complications of radical economic refiguring and structural adjustment taking place in South Africa and beyond. African scholars criticized the neo-Marxist paradigm both for purporting a totalizing model in which actor agency was largely subsumed by the structural and external forces of capitalism and for neglecting African endogenous knowledge and grounded cultural practices (Mafeje 1998). Given *volkekunde's* emphasis on 'culture' as the primordial justification for apartheid's social engineering, most South African social anthropologists viewed the concept antagonistically. During the early period of democratic transition, however, the moratorium placed on 'culture' as an ideological tool of the state began to lift and its relevance as a flexible political and economic resource that enabled people to make meaningful statements about themselves and others was increasingly recognised in ethnographic research (Thornton 1988; Gordon and Spiegel 1993: 96). Anxiety around 'culture' as an analytic persists, however, as its use in claims to rights, heritage, and sovereignty post-apartheid continues to reaffirm its status as a deeply modern *problematique* of anthropology in South Africa as elsewhere (Spiegel 1997; Shepherd and Robins 2008; Comaroff and Comaroff 2009). Other concerns over the exposé style of anthropology that had motivated the UCT department over the last decade had arisen, however, as Gordon and Spiegel (1993) explain:

> ... exposé traditions can be dangerous, particularly when the object of ethnography becomes indictment and challenge only and excludes increasing knowledge and theoretical development. It can also fall into the trap of political correctness where exposé is limited to challenging only one particular political position and deconstructing its rhetoric alone. And it can also produce overly romantic concentrations on resistance and ostracism of those who argue that resistance to apartheid also has its costs. (1993: 89)

The costs of resistance had become clear to academics over the previous decades, most starkly with the assassination of anthropologist David Webster in 1989 for his anti-apartheid activism. Censorship and police harassment were concerns that had driven many anthropologists to leave the country. While the early transition period of the '90s did not see the permanent return of many of these scholars, the lifting of the academic boycott did lead to greater engagement by some American and European anthropologists interested in the human rights conditions of the country's transformation. And, while the opening up of scholarly conversations between the previously isolated departments in South Africa with anthropology in the North America and Europe was seen as an imperative by many of the former to remain relevant and innovative,[13] this growing academic interface also provoked a need for historical introspection. Publications emerged seeking to locate social anthropology within South Africa's recent history and to confront a 'politics of suspicion' that white South African scholars who had remained 'inside' the regime increasingly faced in the international academic community. These works also sought to better gauge where an ethical intervention, if any, would be appropriate post-apartheid.[14]

One scathing critique of South African social anthropology was published by American anthropologist Nancy Scheper-Hughes in her argument for the ethics of a 'militant anthropology' (1995). Directed specifically at the department at UCT where she temporarily occupied a chair and teaching position in 1993/4, Scheper-Hughes presented an image of a department in a state of intellectual paralysis, having withdrawn from the violent and difficult realities of transition to the colonial securities of the

---

[13]Conversations between South African social anthropologists and academics abroad had continued under apartheid, however. Although the academic boycott precluded most scholars from abroad from visiting the country, South African scholars continued to attend international conferences, and people like Colin Murray continued to circumvent the state and sneak into South Africa to continue academic engagement at UCT (Hammond-Tooke 1997: 183 and Spiegel pers comm. April 30*th*, 2014).

[14] See Scheper-Hughes 1995; Robins 1996; Hammond-Tooke 1997; Spiegel 1997; Kuper 1998; Bank and Bank 2013; Spiegel 2005.

tearoom (1995: 415). While Scheper-Hughes's impression that social anthropology had entered into a period of liminality reflects Spiegel's own self-analysis of the time (Gordon and Spiegel 1993: 83), her portrait of an "old order … hanging on to the bitter end", practicing "an evasive microstrategy of resistance" through "*noninvolvement*" (Scheper-Hughes 1995: 415, emphasis hers) both presented an ahistorical perspective of the department's intellectual engagement with state oppression and with poverty in rural sites of relocation and peri-urban townships (described above), and stands in sharp contrast to Spiegel's and others' accounts (Kuper 1995, 1998; Robins 1996; Hammond-Tooke 1997). Moreover, Scheper-Hughes's critique of the 'heroic observer' and her call to South African anthropologists to take action and choose sides overlooks the close similarities between the ANC's and the UCT department's research and teaching imperatives to deconstruct apartheid state propaganda. The department ostensibly *had* chosen sides and was often criticized for allowing politics to direct teaching (Robins 1996: 342). Scheper-Hughes's cry for ethical, yet militant intervention also paints an overly simplistic picture of which parties and individuals participated in the daily violence at the time on political grounds (Kuper 1995: 425; Robins 1996: 341). Indeed, Scheper-Hughes's proposed militant anthropology resembled more closely the stance staunchly taken by the UCT department, including Spiegel, throughout the '80s, a stance that had proven untenable and ethically problematic under the conditions of political transition.

Such moments of intellectual anxiety and uncertainty are not unique to South Africa or to this transitional period in the disciplinary history of anthropology. The relatively late engagement of American anthropology with Marxism has been attributed to political concerns over its proximity to communism after World War II, followed by its eager uptake during the radical social movements that sprang up during the war in Vietnam (Ortner 1984:138-9). Similar concerns over the ethics of engagement and activism by anthropologists were also raised in the keynote address of the 2010 Anthropology Southern Africa (ASnA) conference, held at Fort Hare University, in which anthropologists' stance on recent American military action in the Middle East was raised by Setha

Low, the former president of the American Anthropological Association.[15] I attended this conference shortly before beginning the series of interviews with Spiegel reported on here, and Setha Low's concerns elicited comments and nods of recognition from participants in debates having long since taken place in the tearooms of South African anthropology departments. What had become clear throughout the '90s and well into the following decade was that South African anthropological practice had emerged (and was still emerging) from the particular historical context of the country. Its challenges regarding state opposition, structural inequality and questions of ethical intervention, however, then and now, were not exceptional to South Africa (Gordon and Spiegel 1993: 100).

In addition to the pressing national concerns of the time, many of the analytic and disciplinary questions facing South African, European, and American anthropology departments alike were provoked by a postcolonial and postmodern turn toward a critique of constructions of alterity, Western (especially US) academic hegemony, and a growing inclusion of historically marginalised voices.[16] The anthropologists at UCT recognised that the prospect of institutional transformation, while affirming of the department's scholarly mission, would pose pedagogical challenges.

Both Spiegel (Chapter 5) and Robins (1996) note that, in addition to research, teaching was the predominant form of activism undertaken by most social anthropologists. And while, "for [Robins as] a young white student entering the UCT anthropology department in the early 1980s", the classroom emphasis on deconstructing notions of primordial cultural difference "constituted a powerful critique of apartheid" (1996: 342), the expectation was that the majority of incoming students would no longer be white. The Bantu Education system of apartheid had effectively marginalised black, coloured, and Indian students from

---

[15] See also 'Engaged Anthropology: Diversity and Dilemmas' (Low and Merry 2010).
[16] See Asad 1973; Said 1978; Clifford and Marcus 1986; Keesing 1994; Mafeje 1998; Mbembe 2002; Devisch and Nyamnjoh 2011; Nyamnjoh 2012.

engaging in academic conversations with elite institutions.[17] And while social anthropologists at South African universities had historically given greater voice to the colonised than had other social science disciplines, it is quite a different endeavour to teach ethnography on witchcraft to students for whom witchcraft is a daily fact of life, as opposed to debunking its status as 'backwards superstition' to a majority-white classroom.[18] However, students categorised as 'white', 'African', 'Indian', and 'coloured' alike would still be arriving on UCT's campus having been exposed to apartheid education and the myths of primordialist ethnic distinctions (Robins 1996: 342).[19] The ANC-supported notion of non-racialism was still, therefore, the prevailing message of the day. However, the changing audience would undoubtedly also require a transformation of classroom conversations.

The Postcolonial Turn

Linked closely with this recognition, more general critiques of anthropology also came to the fore. Significant among them was the relative dearth of black African voices among Africanist anthropologists and the question of the discipline's relevance to

---

[17] See Chapter Four for Spiegel's comments about the divisions of universities under apartheid and the few permits and permissions that were granted to students of colour who petitioned to take courses at traditionally white institutions.

[18] This is an example from my own experience leading discussion sections for a first year introductory anthropology course taught by Spiegel. My own tendency had been to teach as I had learned at the University of Illinois, in a classroom primarily composed of white middle-class students from Chicago's suburbs, which was to challenge what seemed to be fairly homogenous assumptions about race, class, and gender. I quickly learned that a different approach was needed in my UCT classroom, which was composed of approximately 50% white students, with a large minority of students, black and white, hailing from Zimbabwe.

[19] The Population Registration Act of 1950 mandated the legal categorization of all South Africans as either 'white', 'coloured' or 'Native', and categories of 'Asian' or 'Indian' were often used to describe 'subgroups' of the 'coloured population'. See Deborah Posel's (2001) 'Race as Common Sense' for an extended discussion of these categories and their gradual implementation by the apartheid state.

independent Africans (Mafeje 1998). South African anthropology had, by this period of transition in the early '90s, produced an impressive yet small cadre of black professional academics including Bernard Magubane, Z.K. Matthews, and Absalom Vilakazi who, like many, had left the country to pursue greater academic freedom during apartheid. Harriet Ngubane and Mamphela Ramphele both held positions in UCT's anthropology department until the mid-'90s, and Ramphele would become UCT's vice chancellor in 1996 (Gordon and Spiegel 1993: 99). Cecil Wele Manona, having briefly held a lectureship in Anthropology at Rhodes University, transferred to Rhodes's Institute of Social and Economic Research in the late 1970s.[20] While the disproportionate number of white academic professionals at English-medium universities would pose an imperative for redress in all departments, the purported expertise of social anthropology on the African experience in the country emphasised the discrepancy in scholarly representation most dramatically.

Archibald Monwabisi Mafeje was an influential black South African scholar who had studied under and published alongside Monica Wilson as a student at UCT in the early '60s. Encouraged by Wilson to pursue post-graduate studies outside South Africa, Mafeje completed a PhD at Cambridge University in 1966 (Sharp 2008; Bank and Bank 2013). He was later selected by an academic committee to be appointed to a teaching position at UCT in 1968, but, under pressure from the Minister of National Education at the time, the university never made him a formal offer (Ntsebeza 2008: 37). This was a decision that provoked student protests across South Africa, constituting, as is revealed below, Spiegel's first contact with anthropology and with protest politics as a young science student at Wits University.[21]

---

[20] Further work is warranted on the history of various black intellectuals in South Africa and elsewhere who were employed as field research assistants but never sufficiently recognised for their analytical contribution in the academy. See chapter eight in Bank and Bank (2013) and the 2008 special edition of the *CODESRIA Bulletin* for a more detailed reflection on Archie Mafeje's experience at the University of Cape Town in the 1960s.

[21] The focus given here to Mafeje stems from his primacy in Spiegel's early experiences with anthropology and politics and is intended to provide greater

Frustrated with academic politics in South Africa, Mafeje went on to establish a celebrated career holding positions in social science departments at both European and African universities. Though he would return to South Africa as a Research Fellow for the National Research Foundation and receive several commendations in the country in his later years (Devisch and Nyamnjoh 2011: 3), his vexed relationship with UCT continued, a matter over which the university would later issue several official apologies amounting to what Olukoshi and Nyamnjoh have called, "too little too late" (2008: 2).

In 1998, Mafeje published a provocative article that posed an acute challenge to the future of Africanist Anthropology titled, 'Anthropology and Independent Africans: Suicide or End of an Era?' Until his death in 2007, Mafeje remained a powerful contributing voice to the critical debates of the late twentieth century concerning anthropology's historical epistemologies of alterity and relationship to colonialism and he staunchly supported the adoption of African endogenous knowledge in the social sciences (Mafeje 2000; Adesina 2008).

Much attention has been given to the postcolonial turn that followed political independence across sub-Saharan Africa, provoking conversations that continue to interrogate, as well as qualify, the significant history and future of anthropology on and in the continent.[22] Other prominent African scholars like V. Y. Mudimbe and the earlier rise of African Nationalist movements across the continent had levelled unsparing critiques against anthropology as "a smokescreen for neo-colonialism" (Nkwi 2007: v). Despite the anxieties and uncertainties of political transition in South Africa and elsewhere, however, or perhaps *because* of them, by the late '80s and '90s the discipline of anthropology had witnessed a new rise in interest on the continent. Established in 1989, the Pan

---

context to the first chapter of interviews to follow. The contributions of African researchers like Livingstone Mqotsi and Godfrey Pitje to South African anthropology, and the critical analyses of Bernard Magubane, for example, deserve further consideration (See Bank and Bank 2013: 6).

[22] See Mbembe 2002; CODESRIA Bulletin 3&4 2008; Devisch and Nyamnjoh 2011; Nyamnjoh 2012.

African Anthropological Association (PAAA), in conjunction with the Council for the Development of Social Science Research in Africa (CODESRIA), was created with the aim of interrogating the direction and viability of the discipline in Africa against the backdrop of such virulent critique. The PAAA and its journal, *The African Anthropologist*, also sought to provide "avenues for critical interchange and exchange amongst anthropologists and other scholars on the continent and beyond" and to identify "the theoretical, epistemological and methodological strengths of the discipline" (Nkwi 2007: vi).

That social anthropology has been shaped by the authority granted to the historically mobile anthropologist as 'knowledgeable outsider' has been rigorously acknowledged by those writing within the discipline since the late twentieth century. However, the difficulties emergent in attempts to include the anthropological gaze of mobile insiders, or those previously considered anthropology's 'subjects' of study, rather than its practitioners, continues to be a topic of much discussion.[23] While Mafeje's call for the "death" of anthropology was premised on compelling arguments that the discipline had reached a kind of terminal stagnation in light of postcolonial critique, its practitioners and students contend that anthropology continues to be transformed by each new generation of scholars and that the discipline wields the tools best suited to its own reinvention. Indeed, Mafeje's career, although difficult at times, is a testament to this point. These debates, however, continue to inform research within and on the postcolony and their thorough acknowledgment is imperative to the continued relevance of anthropology. As Aseka and Murunga (1997), and later Bogopa and Petrus (2007), have explained, African scholars often face double standards of publishing in which they are required to include Africanist texts to demonstrate analytical weight or are often denied journal space, resulting in a disproportionate say by Africanists on things African (Aseka and Murunga 1997: 11). The dialogue that

---

[23] See Clifford and Marcus 1986; Gupta and Ferguson 1992, 1997; Keesing 1994; Ntarangwi 2010; Devisch and Nyamnjoh 2011; Nyamnjoh 2012. It was also predominantly featured at the 2014 Anthropology Southern Africa conference in Grahamstown.

such critique opens up therefore reveals persistent barriers regarding the hegemony of knowledge production.

Anthropologists writing on Africa within the same decade as Mafeje's 'End of an Era', attempting to approach the new challenges posed to their discipline, suggest a number of angles from which to reposition anthropological inquiry. Women feminist theorists and 'halfies', Lila Abu-Lughod has argued (1991), have always conducted research about the 'other' *as* 'others' and have drawn attention to the over-simplification of the binary of insider and outsider (1991: 140-1). Abu-Lughod therefore sought to shift the focus of critique of anthropology away from the position of the researcher toward how the research itself is positioned. She further proposed the use of "ethnographies of the particular" that do not presume to generalise, and thereby to subvert the process of Othering (1991:149). In similar vein, Liisa Malkki presented her ethnography of Hutu refugees in Tanzania not as a study of "a people", but rather "of processes and interconnections" in which she gives considerable attention to history and narrative (1995:1). Sharon Hutchinson's ethnography of dilemmas faced by Nuer communities in Sudan avoids notions of ideal and bounded cultural systems by focusing on "evolving points of confusion and conflict" (1996:28). Finally, Jean and John Comaroff explain that

> ...the epistemic objects of our inquiry are no longer nouns – culture, society, institutions, or whatever – but compound verbs describing the construction and deconstruction of more-or-less stable practices, conventions, forms, commodities, abstractions. (1999:295)

Comaroff and Comaroff further posit that this revision of inquiry accompanies a shift in the scale of anthropology and its consideration of the local *and* the global as analytic constructs (1999:294). This was a reality of which Spiegel and his colleagues were very much aware. The need for the purview of their department to broaden after apartheid became increasingly apparent, as did the necessity to understand South African society as part of a greater global whole, and to be able to work with multilayered interconnections that would again unsettle efforts to conceptualize the unit of analysis.

Anthropology departments persist in South Africa, in many cases merged with departments of sociology. However, their disciplinary autonomy, research methodology, and pedagogy underwent a period of rigorous and often anxious introspection, confronting criticism from both outside and within disciplinary and national borders in the final decade of the twentieth century. Jumping forward to the time of the interviews, in 2011, that are excerpted below, the discipline and department at UCT had become a vibrant space of intellectual discussion and enrichment, one in which critical questions regarding approaches to power, culture, difference, violence, politics, and poverty have remained prominent and where the ground for effectively and ethically planting one's feet in the field and in the classroom has remained unsettled.

20 Years Post-Apartheid: Perspectives from The University of Cape Town, 2010-2014[24]

In an article he co-authored with Robert J. Gordon on the status of South African social anthropology in 1993, Andrew 'Mugsy' Spiegel identified three lacunae of ethnographic research and critical inquiry: violence, ethnicity, and the ruling elite. Endemic violence and ethnic mobilisation were predominant features of regime changeover. The neo-Marxist emphasis on structure, economics and class, while demonstrating the value of grounded qualitative research toward elucidating macro-structures, left the tools for exploring ethnic belonging, personhood, and psychological approaches to trauma underdeveloped (1993: 97-98). And while the term "ruling elite" in Gordon's and Spiegel's report refers most directly to Afrikaner nationalism and governance, a related gap in

---

[24] As stated above in 'conversation starters', the focus here on UCT partly reflects my own bias as a recent UCT student, who became most familiar with the work being produced by faculty between 2009 and 2014. This focus also serves to narrow the discussion to academics linked closely to Spiegel, as a more thorough and broader overview, though warranting greater consideration in future conversations, was not possible here.

scholarly exploration that would be addressed in the early years of the twenty-first century included the interrogation of state apparatuses and policing that had hitherto been considered a pragmatic obstacle for, rather than a frontier of, anthropological inquiry.[25]

Roughly twenty years later, these gaps in South African research have been taken up by a new generation of anthropologists, originating from both inside and outside the country, stimulating inspired new conversations through intellectual exchange. Among current scholars linked directly to Spiegel through his extensive career at UCT is Fiona Ross, who began her undergraduate courses as one of Spiegel's students. Ross's work on gender and 'women' as an emergent category in South Africa's Truth and Reconciliation Commission (TRC) also addressed topics of witnessing, testimony, memory, and violence, all of which had emerged as critical themes of social science research in the country in the decade following apartheid. Additionally, Pamela Reynolds, known for her influential research on childhood in apartheid South Africa (1986; 1989) and who supervised Ross's work on the TRC, has recently published her newest book *War in Worcester* (2013), which explores the role of youth in the anti-apartheid struggle, showing sustained interest in violence, victimisation, memory, and the prolonged pursuit of ethics by the movement's most vulnerable participants. Carolyn Hamilton's pioneering work on archive and public culture has also been significant to the study of memory and history in South Africa. Her efforts to reconfigure the meanings and methodologies of archival research have been seminal in shifting understandings of historical process, the entanglements of pre-colonial, colonial, and postcolonial states and the complex discourses that surround notions of public life.

Other directions in post-apartheid South African social anthropology concern notions of development, scarcity, humanitarianism and health in historically and culturally grounded frameworks. For example, Ross's 2010 monograph, *Raw Life, Now Hope*, was produced from eighteen years of fieldwork following one

---

[25] See Comaroff and Comaroff 2004, 2008.

community's transition from shacks to a 'developed' residential area. Ross traced how people affected by marginalisation and poverty made life-worlds and navigated social possibility under the structural violence of global neoliberalism as it has manifested in the post-apartheid context. Likewise, Patricia Henderson's work on HIV/AIDS and care-giving in rural KwaZulu-Natal (2014) further represents a growing anthropological interest in medical anthropology and the ethics of care under the HIV/AIDS pandemic facing South Africa. Moreover, Susan Levine's research on childhood and child labour addressed in her latest work, *Children of a Bitter Harvest* (2014), and her continued research in medical anthropology, alongside the scholarship of Helen Macdonald, Divine Fuh, Francis Nyamnjoh, and that of their students, demonstrates an emphasis on ethical engagement with interlocutors in precarious situations. Spiegel himself has continued to pursue his interest in development—both its criticism and its possibilities for positive intervention—through his research on waste management in Cape Town's informal settlements (2008, 2010). While emphasizing the complexities and contradictions of agency, subjectivity, conviviality, and power, their research seeks to avoid the pitfalls of so-called 'Afro-pessimism' while offering nuanced insight into the ongoing processes and challenges of social transformations in South Africa.

New areas of research have also emerged, often through a sense of urgency provoked by rapidly changing conditions. For example, Lesley Green's trans-disciplinary endeavours into the relationship between traditional knowledge and science address epistemological quandaries that have arisen in fields of marine science, biodiversity conservation, climate change and ethics. Green's work, and that of her students, is forging connections with 'critical humanities' that aim to retheorise how we approach knowledge itself and is broadening the horizons of anthropological research. Between the time of these interviews in 2011 and their reporting here in 2014, my own post-graduate cohort at UCT has produced original research related to tuberculosis treatment procedures and policies; the roles of NGOs and a privatizing sector of international aid and development; contested knowledge and political ecology in Western

Cape fishing communities; discourse and contestation over governance and the delivery of services and infrastructure promised under the new constitution; the persistence and intensification of poverty; the growth of culture commoditisation in the tourism and heritage industries; the nation-building projects and politics of sport; the use of information and communication technologies by migrant workers, foreign nationals, refugees, women, and youth; the everyday ethics and aspirations of sustainability in permaculture communities; the negotiation of gendered and LGBTQI identities in social space; and the intermittent outbreak of xenophobic violence in the country coinciding with hardening notions of ethnicity, autochthony, and new modes of economic exclusion.

Yet, new directions do not mean the end of old problems. In 2011, there was heated debate among humanities post-graduates at UCT regarding the administration's decision to "disestablish" the Centre for African Studies (CAS). Never envisioned as a closure, "disestablishment" was rather invoked as a precursor to merging CAS with the departments of social anthropology, linguistics, and the African Gender Institute into what came to be called simply "the new school", and more formally, "The School of African and Gender Studies, Anthropology and Linguistics" (coded and then known as AXL). While the administrative move maintained the distinctive operations of each department alongside creating channels for greater interdisciplinary dialogue and research, news that CAS might "close" elicited an outcry from students concerned that the department's critical perspective on 'Africa' as an academic signifier was no longer being taken seriously by the university. The controversy climaxed after an article entitled 'UCT in war over "bantu education"' appeared in *The Mail&Guardian* newspaper with parallels drawn with the infamous 'Mamdani Affair': a reference to a dispute in 1997 between the newly appointed director of CAS, Mahmood Mamdani, and UCT's then Social Science Faculty administration (Spiegel included) over a draft syllabus for a foundational course on the study of Africa (Macfarlane 2011).

The contention and hyperbole over the departmental merger eventually dissipated, however, and 'the new school' was launched in 2012 without any changes to faculty or course-offerings. And yet, the impassioned dialogue evoked by the university's move to reorganise disciplinary boundaries also showed that social anthropology was still a discipline viewed with suspicion by many in South African academia, especially those concerned with critical inquiry into the multivalent meaning of 'Africa'. Pointing further to the complexity of the debate, the committee that recommended the merger was chaired by Francis Nyamnjoh, then Head of the Department of Social Anthropology at UCT. Nyamnjoh's subsequent publication, 'Blinded by Sight' (2012b), addressed what many saw as precisely that suspicion of anthropology as practised in Africa.[26] Such controversies also demonstrate that a chronological accounting of institutional histories, like the one I have attempted to provide here, can present a deceptive narrative. Universities in South Africa, as elsewhere, do not simply progress toward better knowledge-making practices. Rather, they emerge in complex ways within their wider social, national, and global contexts in which the past and the future haunt the present. Old questions find new relevance and new questions reveal familiar challenges.

Moreover, UCT's development of 'the new school' also raises questions as to the distinctiveness of the involved departments' disciplinary focus and methodology. Gordon and Spiegel's (1993) uncertainty concerning the future of anthropology as an autonomous discipline in South Africa therefore remains in question, as the themes of anthropology's new scholarly purview are increasingly taken up by other departments. Cross-border-linking therefore continues to be an ongoing project of UCT's anthropologists, between disciplines institutionally and also between institutions internationally, pursued with varying degrees of uncertainty and tenacity regarding the discipline's future.

---

[26] Nyamnjoh has emphasized that his article 'Blinded by Sight' (2012b) constitutes the second half of a two-part conversation. The first part of this conversation was outlined in his piece 'Potted Plants in Greenhouses' (2012a) in which he addresses in greater detail his central point about "the epistemological and social implications of knowledge production in Africa" (Nyamnjoh 2013: 127).

Questions for the Future

South African anthropology continues to be shaped by the particular histories, inheritances, struggles, and shifting grounds that characterise the country's ceaseless becoming. While emerging from a transnational history of British social theory, more sociological than cultural in orientation, South African social anthropology's particular embeddedness in its own field site of inquiry (unlike departments in Euro-America that have historically studied 'elsewhere'), and its co-evolution within, and in reaction to, an oppressive state have afforded it a unique perspective. Though still situated, as UCT is, in the proverbial 'ivory tower' of academia, perched monumentally against an iconic mountain in the heart of an apartheid-planned city, with a student body still disproportionally white, it cannot be called a European university. Nor is South African anthropology a European discipline. Its intellectual positionality and scholarly perspective are uniquely South African. And, like South Africa, its anthropologists are experiencing an ongoing and radical reordering of things in the Foucauldian sense. This reorganisation of meanings, mobilities, possibilities, and desires are not exceptional to South Africa, as emphasised above, but characteristic of a more global late-modernism.

Critical theorists across disciplines have pointed to the ways in which economic neoliberalism with its impetus toward privatisation, de-regulation, and the ever-expanding reach of the market into new domains and across borders are having profound implications for human subjectivity (Harvey 2005; Ferguson 2006). For Appadurai (1990), there is something "strikingly new" about the interactivity of the (post-)modern world. "The forces of cultural gravity" that previously "seemed always to pull away from the formation of large-scale ecumenes" (1) has changed. A "technological explosion" has occurred, not only in transportation, but also through digital forms of media that instantly circulate information and images constituting new configurations of "cultural traffic". And yet, this new gravitational field of more freely flowing ideas, images, and capital has proven to have the paradoxical effect of both liberating and constricting notions of place. New fields of possibility provoke new desires and drive (or coerce) movement, but the experience of this new mobility, for most, has been one of disjuncture rather than flow (1990: 1-6).

As states increasingly open their borders to new flows of capital, they simultaneously harden the boundaries of belonging and citizenship (Nyamnjoh 2006; Geschiere 2009). Agents of the de-territorializing state remain nervous that the imagined community constituting the front half of the hyphenated nation-state is threatened from various, racialised Others (Appadurai 1990: 13-14). For some, innovation, ingenuity and new avenues of entrepreneurialism paved by culture industries, heritage tourism, and *Ethnicity, Inc.*, will find various configurations of the self-stylised and ethnicised self as a resource available for commoditisation and market participation (Comaroff and Comaroff 2009). For most, the new desires and expectations shaped by increasingly visible forms of spectacular wealth results in greater frustration at the growing impossibility of the majority to capture and actualise them (Comaroff and Comaroff 1999). Finally, further concerns revolve around new and gendered modes of racialised exclusion in the growing desperation to do so (See Nyamnjoh 2006; Sharp 2008; Sichone 2008).

Twenty years after apartheid, theorists are still creating vocabularies to describe the effects of the neoliberal reorganisation of both capital and people that has characterised political transition. The distinctive characteristics of late-capitalism in South Africa, for Achille Mbembe, following Fanon, emerge from the historical methodologies of brutality and social control practised under colonialism and apartheid (2008, 2011, 2012, 2013). Spiegel and his colleagues spent a significant portion of their careers ascertaining key features of how apartheid's governance involved weakening black people's capacity to reproduce family life through the migrant labour system, the dispossession of land, and forced relocation into partitioned and regulated spaces of scarcity. Moreover, the agents of apartheid enforced a bodily form of brutality and the resulting corporeal fear tended to deplete its victims' capacity to imagine, to aspire, "to engage in meaningful symbolic and creative work" (Mbembe 2013: 3).

While the end of apartheid removed these state apparatuses, induction into the emerging neoliberal world order that coincided with South Africa's move to democracy meant less a transition to 'freedom', in the liberal-humanist sense, than to the freedom to consume. And yet, the context of impoverishment has not changed under the new global neoliberal order for the majority of South Africa's people. Rather, a kind of recoding of states of misery, debt and precarity has taken place. Mbembe therefore asks: what can democracy, as the freedom to choose and the freedom to consume, mean to a materially poor and property-less majority (2012, 2013)?

Along with the growing contradiction of citizenship based on consumption and the persistent inability for so many to consume—compounded by new mediascapes that shape new desires—other disappointments about the New South Africa have emerged. First is the increasing doubt regarding South Africa's exceptionalism, noted also in 1993 by Gordon and Spiegel (1993: 100), as the status of the 'rainbow nation' as a beacon of democratic transition and reconciliation has been called starkly into question. Second is the realisation that South Africa's 'miracle' or 'Mandela moment' was in fact a stalemate. Moreover, the aspiration of a non-racial society has proven excessively complicated. While the primacy of race continues to undergo a symbolic reorganisation in meaning, entangled with shifting vectors of class, gender, status, autochthony, and sexuality, the modes of capitalist production in South Africa continue to rely on what Mbembe has called "racial discounts" (2012). The migrant labour of the mining industries and the pools of domestic labour vying to serve middle and upper-class households has not become any whiter, for example.

As a result, the impression of South Africa's present is still, to many and in many ways, one of stagnation. Yet, as Mbembe argued in a lecture given at Harvard University in 2013, this seemingly 'stationary state' is deceptive. "Below the surface, a decisive struggle is unfolding", yet its potential and direction remain unclear *(pers comm. 9 Sept 2013)*. The challenge for South African anthropologists, like Spiegel, who recognise these changes and their many detriments, remains the question of where to insert themselves as social scientists with a history of theoretical approaches of a decisively combative bent. Neoliberalism does not offer an easily visible or definable enemy to battle.

In my most recent conversation with Spiegel since the conclusion of our interviews, he expressed a similar sense of "stagnation" as to the present reordering of things. "People are busy rearranging the deck chairs", he explained. "The ship on the sea has stopped moving, but the crew are rearranging the chairs to create the appearance that they are still going somewhere" (*pers comm. 22 Jan, 2014*). Both Mbembe's and Spiegel's metaphors point to the free-floating forms of control under which familiar methods of discipline utilised by the state, and in the struggle, are in crisis, but on which the ruling political elite have been able to capitalise (Mbembe 2013). Might it be that familiar tactics of social control are being disguised by the new and disorienting circumstances of neoliberal uncertainty? If so, might the 2012 massacre of striking miners at Marikana, the episodes of police brutality that have been increasingly reported, the shadow economies of corruption, and the return of appeals to 'tradition' and 'culture' in response to, among other things, a new 'peril' of alternative sexualities, be examples of apartheid-era disciplines (re)emerging anew? If so, might there be a (re)emerging space for combative theory-making that seeks to reveal the links between individual suffering, state violence, and the macro-economic and political structures relevant to the wider world? The dire circumstances of disposable populations, perhaps energizing beneath the surface of seeming stagnation, lends a pressing urgency to social theory that can speak to power with the nuance and complexity of grounded research. If things are not as new as they appear to be, Spiegel's story may have considerably more value to social theory than its archive.

Conclusion: A Good Foot Soldier

Andrew 'Mugsy' Spiegel partly attributes his coming to anthropology to his uncertain maneuvering through academia, his volunteer work in Lesotho, and his stint on a Kibbutz in Israel which he had claimed was a period of study abroad, in order to avoid military service in South Africa. Humble, but never reticent,

Spiegel also explained in our interviews that he does not think he will be particularly remembered for his contributions to anthropology. In a recent conversation, however, Francis Nyamnjoh—an enthusiastic proponent of this project—described his colleague as a "devoted foot soldier" of the discipline. While he is neither a self-professed captain nor a lieutenant of the long-fought and complex academic battle against apartheid, the metaphors of combat and foot-soldiering suit Spiegel well. And no battle is won without its foot soldiers.

Andrew Spiegel fought apartheid with his weapons of choice: innovative research, theory targeted to deconstruct state knowledge/power, and an aggressive pedagogy that has earned him a reputation for admonishing uncritical scholarship. He remained an advocate of anthropology in South Africa throughout a tumultuous period when its defence was not always popular and he continues to take that stance. While remaining devoted to anthropology and the institutions that gave him the tools to think critically about his own society and dedicated to passing on those tools to his students, Spiegel is also well aware of the complex structures linking knowledge production, political ideology, and state power. Though an invaluable foot soldier for anthropology in South Africa, deploying critical theory to combat state propaganda, Spiegel has never, in fact, been militant. There were periods of institutional uncertainty when his efforts kept the Department of Social Anthropology at UCT viable. Yet, rather than policing disciplinary boundaries, or striving to preserve some sense of territorial sovereignty, Spiegel's tactics have involved keeping social anthropology in South Africa relevant and innovative through academic conversation and cross-border-linking. He has worked hard over the years to recruit scholars with broad interests to invigorate UCT's anthropology department and challenge its students. Through his involvement with ASnA, the PAAA, as well as the International Union of Anthropological and Ethnological Sciences (IUAES) and the World Council of Anthropological Associations (WCAA), he has forged connections with and between anthropologists across the globe and helped to bolster the discipline's postcolonial relevance across the African continent, and the visibility of South Africa-based anthropologists in the global community of anthropologists.

There are few people who share the same kind of groundedness that Spiegel holds in a discipline predicated upon context and qualitative research. His institutional insights make him an excellent interlocutor, historian, and anthropologist of South African anthropology and an extremely engaged one at that. Although Spiegel has not published as widely, or claimed the same notoriety as some of the anthropologists mentioned above, his contribution to social anthropology in South Africa is phenomenal. His story offers a unique perspective from the center of the recent history of anthropology in South Africa, yet from the insightful peripheries of its more commonly known narrative. As a scholar, teacher, administrator, and colleague, the value of his experience to the kind of intergenerational conversations presented here is immeasurable and sharing it with his students remains an integral part of his own anthropological practice.

Prefatory Comment

The following comprise a collection of partial transcripts of a set of open-ended interviews, conducted between April and June 2011, in which Andrew 'Mugsy' Spiegel was free to range across as wide a variety of concerns as his thoughts raised. They do not constitute either a biography or a set of memoirs since there was no strict narrative plot line either to the interview process or to the selections taken for inclusion here, although the latter has followed some broad thematic chronology. What is presented here has been reviewed by Spiegel for comment and annotation, as is increasingly the practice in anthropology and oral history. Spiegel has made further edits in places where he felt that ensuring the privacy of colleagues and acquaintances required revision in a published version. Finally, I have chosen to label Spiegel's dialogue with the name 'Mugsy' (or 'M') rather than 'Andrew' or 'Spiegel', as Mugsy is the name most commonly used to refer to him by both his friends and colleagues. And, while matching the conversational tone of the following interviews, it is also the name by which I have known him since he became my professor in 2009.

Chapter 1

Finding Politics …

When we spoke last, Mugsy had shown me a scrapbook of newspaper clippings from his days as an undergraduate at Wits that his mother had made for him. He had started studying the sciences at university but, looking back, his participation in a petition and demonstration concerning the University of Cape Town's treatment of anthropologist Archie Mafeje had been what first ignited his political and anthropological consciousness.
He pointed out a particular photograph from a newspaper article that pictured five beleaguered-looking young men with shaved heads. They had been hazed by a group of students from Pretoria University for demonstrating in support of Mafeje. He asked me if I could tell which one was him. After several seconds of intent staring, I picked the right young man.

Jess: What year was that?

Mugsy: Nineteen … sixty-eight?

J: Why did you switch to anthropology?

M: *Why* did I get into anthropology?

J: Yeah, why did you switch from science?

M: The switch from science is a different answer than the switch to anthropology. But in order to answer that, I need to tell you how I ended up in science.

I was middle-class, from the northern suburbs of Johannesburg. I was a middle-class Jewish boy. I was going to go into business with my father. [First] I had to do military service the year after I finished high school. Nine months. And at the end of that I had three or five months to kill. I was always going to do commerce; I

1

always thought that was where I was going. I worked for my father for three or four months. During that time I suddenly realised that this commerce thing wasn't going to work for me. I had worked and I had done a lot of jobs as an accountant—an auditing clerk—which I did on school holidays. That was fine, but being in the business ... I kind of looked at it and I ... I didn't recognise the problem as one of accumulation. I couldn't understand—well I didn't—I couldn't have phrased it that way. But I looked at it and I thought, why does anybody work as hard as this to make money? In order to invest it to make more money? And then invest *that* to make even more money? That just didn't make a whole lot of sense to me. I didn't know why. I didn't understand the accumulative principle. Anyway, [I travelled] around the countryside for a couple of weeks with a school friend of mine who had left high school around the same time as me but had managed to avoid army call up. He also didn't know what he wanted to do. His parents were pushing him into medicine, and he convinced me that that was where I should go.

But it was too late for me to get into the medical faculty. My school results would have gotten me in if I had applied in time. So I did the equivalent to the first year of medical courses, which at that stage was physics, chemistry, botany, and zoology .... So I signed up for those in Science. I dropped botany, failed zoology, and passed the chemistry and physics. And then I decided chemistry was where I was going to go, because now there was another friend of mine, whom I had met in the army and [had become] close to at Wits, and *he* was doing chemistry. The medical friend of mine is now a leading rheumatologist in Britain. The chemist, the other friend, became a chemist, a PhD and now runs a business in Boston. And he was convinced that he was going to become a chemist. And so I thought, "that's where it's at for me". And I had done reasonably well in the chemistry first year course, so I went on with that. I did maths and applied maths—that was required for a major in chemistry—and I did well in the first year maths and applied maths. And the second year chemistry I failed because I wasn't actually interested. Because ... why was I doing it!? Because

2

... I didn't know—I didn't know what I was going to do with my life.

J: What year in university were you then?

M: That was my first year. I was a completely naïve, middle-class kid. And I kind of had been brought up in a relatively liberal ... eh, not liberal ... what was then called the Progressive Party: Helen Suzman's party. And that was the constituency in which I lived. Those were the ideas that my parents had and I'd never thought much about them.

So, I then went on to university, and then I heard of this man called Mafeje who was offered a job at UCT, and then was denied it. And the Wits students, where I was, decided to have a protest. We had permission to walk ... to march through the streets, and then permission was rescinded—or revoked—and we drew up a petition. And I was just a first-year student. I mean I had no leading role in this. We signed the petition, and then the guys who put the petition together, who were SRC [Students' Representative Council] leaders, asked for anybody who had motor cars. We were protesting on the side of the road at the time, at the edge of the campus. And you'll see some of those photographs in the same collection—of paint being thrown at us, and that sort of stuff. [The SRC leaders] asked everybody who had a motor car to bring them up and get a convoy together and drive the petition to Pretoria to the prime minister, who was then in residence. I had a motor car. So, I picked it up and ... two of my friends, plus one other guy I didn't know and his girlfriend, got into the car. So there were five of us in the car. And ... we drove ... in convoy to Pretoria. The guys with the petition went ahead [in another car] because they realised the convoy was going to go too slowly—because convoys only go as fast as the slowest car—and they wouldn't have gotten to the Union Buildings before the prime minister had gone home for his afternoon scotch.

J: So the convoy itself was a kind of protest ...

M: The convoy lumbered along slowly toward Pretoria. We got to this entrance and the traffic police stopped us and said, "you can't go into the city. It's half past four in the afternoon", or thereabouts, "and you can't go into the city. It's rush hour time and you're in a convoy without permission" ... And I just said to everybody else—to all the other drivers—"well get back in your cars, switch your lights off, and we'll meet at the Union Buildings". But the others didn't move so fast, so my car got through Pretoria—to the Union Buildings—ahead of any of the others in the convoy. The guys who had carried the petition had gone, had handed it over, and left. There are also photographs of that. We got there, and there were hundreds of Pretoria students waiting for us. And so, that incident happened ... we got beaten up and shaved and stuff.

J: And what did they throw on you? Paint?

M: There were five of us in the car. They split us [up]. They took two in other cars and they made me drive my car to a [student residence hall], where we met the others. One of the people in my car was a girl and they wouldn't do anything or harm her in any way. They had ... old fashioned chivalry ... and they managed to establish that she had an aunt of some kind in Pretoria and so on the way to the residence we drove past her aunt's place and she got out. They took the rest of us—that was four: two in the other car and two that rode with me—to their residence and they shaved us top and bottom, put us in and out of cold showers and put polish all over us. And it was August, so ...

J: It was cold.

M: It was cold! Um ... and then—amazing—what was absolutely astonishing was that another close friend—as I said there were two close friends of mine there, in fact the chemist was one of them, the one that is now in Boston—and astonishingly there was

4

another [friend] who had hung around the suburbs together with us, who suddenly showed up at this residence as well! He was also being beaten up and shaved. He had arrived a little bit later in another car, with a Frenchman and two women, and they wouldn't touch the women again. And the Frenchman managed to talk his way out of anything because ... "touch me and you've got an international incident on your hands" ... so they had dragged this one friend [of the other three of us]; and it was amazing that there he was too! And he hadn't been in my car, so—other than another friend of ours that wasn't at university and made up our suburban friendship group of five—the four of us [who used to hang around the suburbs together] were suddenly together! With this one outsider in this instance, the fellow who'd asked to accompany us with his girlfriend ...

Anyway, that's irrelevant in terms of what you're asking. But what it did was made me—all of us, actually—kind of question protest politics. But it also then led me to kind of ... interpret the situation. I started asking much more intense questions about the politics of the country. I mean, the Progressive Party was one that believed in—which had as part of its platform: 'qualified franchise'. If you're intelligent and educated, and knew what franchise was, and could make an intelligent vote and be rational about it because your education enabled you to, then you should vote. And of course, Archie Mafeje was intelligent and rational and educated, so—well, *because* he was educated—of course, he needed to have a right to have a job at UCT. But the political position wasn't ... it meant that the majority of the country's population would not have had the vote by that policy. It also would have excluded a whole lot of people that I ended up in the army with, who were white, but who were so poorly educated that they were clearly and completely irrational, in my mind. So, it was certainly not a universal franchise position. This incident completely shifted me.

But the fact that Mafeje was an anthropologist was completely irrelevant to my experience at that point. He had been a student here [at UCT] ...

J: Yes, and then he went to Cambridge. Monica Wilson told him he should go there to do his PhD.

M: Which she did with most of her students, almost none of them did PhDs here. Martin West was an exception. And I suspect that was because Martin had obligations here, or something. I'm not sure why he didn't go to Cambridge. I never asked him.

But ... while Mafeje was finishing his PhD, he applied for a job here [at UCT], and from what I understand the selection committee decided to make him the offer. It became public knowledge, but at that point any offer of any appointment had to be approved by the University Council.

J: So this selection committee was made up of—

M: —of academics

J: So it wasn't just anthropologists?

M: No, it wouldn't have just been anthropology. Selection committees, even now, [would be] members of the department plus members of other departments, chaired by the Deputy Dean. It was the same sort of arrangement. And, what happened was, it was made public that he was going to get the offer; that the committee had made that decision.

Archie had been fairly active politically as well, with the PAC as I understand it, and in the New Unity Movement. And the state got to hear about it. The minister of ... I think of education or police—this is all recorded somewhere—said it wasn't permissible and put pressure on the university council, through the vice chancellor, not to make an offer. And so, no offer was actually formally made. But because it was public knowledge, students at the time here [at UCT] then mobilised and had a sit-in in what is now called The Mafeje Room in the Bremner building [UCT central administration building]. And because of that, there is this big metal barricade—if you go there late afternoon you'll see that at five o'clock or four o'clock, whenever they close the place, they drop a big metal

6

barricade so you can't just get into the Bremner building ... The sit-in went on [for over a week].

So that's the bit about Mafeje.

J: So had you been interested in politics before?

M: Eh, peripherally ... peripherally.

J: Were your parents Progressive Party members?

M: My parents ... my father probably was. My mother always voted for Helen Suzman, because it was all constituency-based at that stage. Um, but ... she was a little bit more left-thinking than that, but not massively. My grandmother, I think, was—my maternal grandmother. But she died when I was seven years old. My maternal grandfather was an artisan and a unionist, so he read the union-type literature. But he wasn't an activist, just a union member. And my father was a businessman, very standard middle class stuff, and he had grown up in that sort of family as well, in Germany.

J: So this had been your first protest, the motorcade at Wits?

M: Oh Absolutely! But it made me question protest politics, which doesn't mean I haven't got involved in more since. I got involved with this thing called South African Voluntary Service (SAVS)—[those of us] that got our hair shaved did. There we were, sort of ... "What can we do"? It had made us aware of problems in a way that we hadn't realised. We found this organisation and got involved—they used to go out and build schools and clinics. It was patronizing stuff! But it had a very significant other side to it. We would go in groups of fifteen or twenty students, spend weekends and very often during [university vacations]—three weeks away in Lesotho, Swaziland, and Botswana.

In South Africa, it was hard to find a place where you could do that without having to get permission from the state first, other than on farms. There was a farm outside of Jo'burg [Bronkhorstspruit] … it was the first ever place I went [on one of these] weekends. We went there … and then I went to Lesotho and Botswana and others went to Swaziland over longer periods. We then came into contact with black people as people, not as servants, service workers, or cleaners, or as petrol attendants. And we also … being together … we kind of talked about these sorts of things, and it kind of politicised us. So that politicised me and made me think about these sorts of questions …

And then the science [at university] wasn't working. I mean, I told you I failed the chemistry II. I repeated the chemistry, because my parents said "keep at it". I did maths II and applied maths II, and I failed the whole lot by the end of that year … because by that point I realised it wasn't going to work for me. It wasn't what I wanted to do. So I then had this idea that I wanted to get into development—whatever that meant.

J: Did you think you knew what it meant at the time?

M: No, I had no idea. I just wanted to go and do that type of work on a full-time basis—work that I'd experienced some of with SAVS—is what I had imagined, I suppose. And more to formally work with organisations that did that sort of stuff.

J: As a way to help people?

M: Yeah, to, you know … better life for all—that idea. But that [ANC] slogan wasn't around at the time. At the end of that third year at Wits, I realised that it was pointless to continue. I had been convinced by a number of friends … Again, I was a northern suburbs Jewish boy. I'd been sent to a Methodist school, so I wasn't part of the suburban South African Jewish community, but I came back into that and there's a very strong Zionist presence amongst Jewish South Africans. I'd never been brought up with that, partly because my parents are western Europeans and not eastern Europeans. They objected to the '*shtetl*' mentality, as they called it, of the Lithuanian Jews all around us. Um, but I got caught up in

8

some of the Zionist stuff. My friends were sort of in the Zionist movement, and they said: "look you're having a rough time. Go to Israel. That's where you're going to find your home". And the one friend of that five, the one who didn't come to university and missed having his head shaved and boot polished, actually still lives in Israel.

Spiegel and peers after being beaten, forced into and out of cold showers, shaved and smeared with shoe polish by Pretoria University students. Spiegel far right. 1968. © 2014 Times Media Limited/DALRO, South Africa.

Spiegel back centre, arms crossed. 1968. Originally printed in Hoofstad, permissions granted by CPT Limited.

Chapter 2

Coming to Anthropology

"In a sense, I became an anthropologist because I was running away from military service. It was kind of weird, if I think about it"

J: Did you go to Israel?

M: I went to Israel, after a while.

J: Did you find your home there?

M: No. No, I went travelling, first to Europe. I sort of wandered around and then went to Israel to learn Hebrew and work on a Kibbutz in the middle of 1971. A Kibbutz is a communal farm. When they started, they were very much socialist. They're not anymore.

J: And that was in the '60s?

M: They started in the '30s I think, or '40s. They started before the formation of the state of Israel. I don't know the full history of the Kibbutz, really, but the one I was on was still run then on fundamentally socialist lines. A generation of children who had grown up there was objecting to having to have their children brought up in children's homes. Because what had happened in that earlier generation—adults had children, but then they'd put the children into, kind of, big dormitories. Of course they looked after their own children. Mothers were involved there, but it meant that they got on with their other work and children were brought up as part of a commune rather than each pair of parents looking after their children. Those children who grew up that way objected.

By the time I was there those children's homes were being closed down and parents were caring for children in their own small houses.

J: ...a social experiment that didn't work out—

M: The second generation didn't like it. And initially the older generation objected to changing. [The younger generation] then just left to settle on another Kibbutz nearby where it was possible to do what they wanted. And so the older generation suddenly realised they were going to lose their whole Kibbutz; it would fall apart because there was no one to keep it going. So, even though they were still in the majority, they had to accept that change. They were coerced by their children.

Anyway, I went there, partly because I thought that I might learn from the Kibbutz experience about setting up similar kinds of things in South Africa. But I soon realised that wasn't going to work, because what drove the Kibbutz was the kind of nationalist zeal that underlies Zionism, and which I was only too pleased to get out of. So after seven months in Israel, [five and a half] of them on a Kibbutz, I left to come back [to South Africa] and study—so that I could do the courses that were needed to get into development. On the way home, I went a sort of roundabout way via England. And I met, through a friend—in fact the medical friend, the one that became a doctor—through his sister who was in England at the time; she was very close friends with the leader of the sit-in, or one of the two leaders of the sit-in—a guy called Raphie Kaplinsky—who had gone into that development stuff, and he still works in that field. I met him and I explained what I was doing and what I wanted to do. He was then a PhD student at Sussex. I said, "what courses should I do at UCT in order to find myself where you are"? And he said, "economics, economic history, an African language, and anthropology" ... And I discovered it!

I had no idea. I had been in one lecture once, because of one of my friends at Wits who was doing anthropology and was completely in awe—like everybody in his class was, particularly the women—of one lecturer called John Blacking. He was a good-

14

looking man, and also a very eloquent and charismatic figure. He used to take students on field trips to Botswana ... [My friend] took me to one of his classes once because she said that I would be excited by it. I remember going and not being particularly turned on by it. ... And I didn't connect him with Archie Mafeje when that [demonstration] happened. It was just a friend's class, which I went to because she was excited and thought it was a good thing to attend. But I didn't make any connections, this may have been later even, that I went to her class, after the Mafeje incident. I'm not sure, a year or two later ...

What happened was, I had planned to do the economics and go that route. But ... I had not wanted to be in business, and all I got from the first-year economics course was business! And I kind of fought with my economics tutor. I think in a year-long course there was one lecture on socialist economics and one lecture on what they thought was primitive economics—on barter or something— and for the rest it was just supply and demand curves, and I just hated it!

[Speaking now of anthropology:], at that stage, photocopying was very expensive and hardly available, and the first-year social anthropology class had grown too large to fit into A-100 in my year, '72, which was my first year here [at UCT]. And the department decided to break the class up into six different cohorts, alphabetically. They had six essays throughout the year and I as an 'S' ended up having to do essay number four, which was the economic anthropology essay, at the beginning of the year long course. Because we just rotated though the topics, they weren't linked to the lectures. You did the reading, you wrote the essay and got some advice from your tutor, but your lectures were going on at a different rate, around different issues. And so my first ever essay was on economic anthropology. And I read this stuff and I thought, but this is what I want to learn! And I wrote an essay—Sally Frankental was my tutor.

I wrote this essay and I also included some stuff about the Kibbutz, because, you know, reciprocity and redistribution and all that stuff—the Kibbutz was a wonderful example! And of course, Sally being the Zionist she is, she was completely taken by the fact

15

that not only was I reading beyond what was required, and doing a good job, but that I also was thinking outside of that and introducing my own experience in Israel. So my mark was really high, and I was hooked!

So that's how I came to anthropology, and I've stuck with it since. I also did African History, but that wasn't a full major at the time. So I did anthropology; as much as I could do at an undergrad level. And I also became particularly fascinated with Lesotho through the South African Voluntary Service (SAVS) stuff, so I would go there every vacation ... And I was also having to avoid more military service, because they used to make us go for more camps. We went for nine month for basic [training]. And then we used to have to go ... at least once a month for a Tuesday evening or Saturday afternoon thing and also to three or four week camps, once every couple of years.

J: You had to do that even though you were a university student?

M: And then they wanted you to go on three-week camps, either in July or over the summer holiday. I went on one of those in 1969, *after* I'd hit the front page of *The Rand Daily Mail* with the hair-shaved thing [from when I participated in the demonstration at Wits], and I was treated like ... uh, I don't know, like a criminal. There were five of us who were singled out for special treatment on that three-and-a-half-week camp—two of us from Wits who were regarded as political activists and three guys who had spent time in prison. The camp was held in Potchefstroom. In the freezing cold, I lay in a tent outside Potchefstroom listening to the radio as the first moon landing occurred. Freezing my butt, but listening to this little radio we had.

Anyway, there were five of us singled out. Another fellow who'd been politically active at Wits in some sort of way, I've forgotten how, but he was a Wits student. The two of us, and three hardened criminals—I mean, they were real hardened criminals—were singled out for special treatment. And after those three or four weeks I decided I wasn't going to touch the army again. I mean, I hadn't wanted to be in it anyway. I just kind of went along, and didn't think too hard about what I was doing. But after that I wasn't going to go near it again.

J: So you only did one of these camps—

M: You were supposed to do them for initially what was supposed to be three years after you'd finished high school. Nine months of basic, and I think in the following three years you had to do another two of those camps, and also the Saturday afternoon things. And Tuesday nights as well … I did some of those, and then [the state] kind of cut back on that, though it increased the number of camps and the period over which one was obligated to do them. And then I went to Israel. I think I got a letter, but I wrote to them and said, "look, I'm going to be out of the country for the next three years … studying … or four years", I don't know precisely what I said; something like that. And I got two or three years of leave, and so I didn't have to bother [about army camps]. When I came back after just one year they fortunately didn't connect, uh— the passport control people didn't tell the army I was back—so I had a couple years of grace.

But near the end of that time, they wanted me back again. So I kept going to Lesotho, saying, "No, I have to be doing this research, it's part of my studies, I haven't got time to" … And I kept on going to Lesotho basically to avoid the army. So it was kind of an escape, but I was also learning Sesotho. I was hanging around and just being part of the place, and becoming an anthropologist! In a sense, I became an anthropologist because I was running away from military service. It is kind of weird, if I think about it now.

J: And these camps were surely segregated as well? You were only in a camp with other whites?

M: You haven't understood. There were no blacks in the army. There were black people who were linked to the army—they weren't just segregated within the forces; they were segregated from the rest because, simply phrased, there were no blacks at all in the

17

army. There was a small coloured unit, I think. They had a base here near Macassar. You can still see Faure base as you drive along the N2 toward Somerset West, there's a little military base there. That was a coloured unit. And there were black cleaners. But they weren't soldiers.

In '67, I was involved with the first ... well, I was in a very small unit, seventy or eighty guys—it was an electronic reconnaissance unit. It was linked with the artillery, but I was never involved with the guns, other than having to clean them as punishment. I was a radar operator, working with this little—not little—a big trailer that got hauled behind a truck; Second World War design—British—that got hauled behind a truck and then got positioned somewhere in the veld. You had to then plot it in by taking coordinates from beacons and stuff, and know exactly where it was. If mortars were fired by the enemy, you would be told by people up at the front ... your listening/observation post was up front. I'd be waiting up there at this machine for communications from the guys at the listening post. As soon as we were told mortars were being fired we had to switch on the machine. Its batteries did not last very long—car batteries. And you could then see the mortar as a blip go up over the screen, and you marked it on this little thing, and then you raised the radar a little higher. You'd raise it faster than the mortar actually travelled, and you'd get another blip on the screen. And then somehow the computer, which took up most of this machine and was probably nowhere near as powerful as my laptop—but it was a machine half the size of this room I suppose ... you'd punch in—you'd sort of mark out where that was. We placed some little hairline markers on the screen. And you'd thus tell the computer where you'd seen these two blips, and how long it had taken between the two. I think it recorded, because you pressed a button each time, and it could tell you where it had been fired from within five or six metres. So then you could tell your own artillery where to fire onto.

So that was what I was involved in. And there were others in the unit—the people, the listening post people, up on the front— they also had radio systems where they put out microphones across the veld in different places, widespread. And they had a way of working with how long the sound of fire from different microphones took to come from a certain point, and they could then work out, again approximately, where that was coming from and then aim their own guns on that point. And then there was a straight surveying section, surveying all these things in. Um, but that was basically what I was in.

Now, that little unit was used to set up ... an exercise: the first ever anti-guerilla exercise, or what was called manoeuvre, in the country. Near the Botswana border ... where there was a military base ... our unit of eighty people was made into the terrorists. We had to roam around the bush in groups of not more than four or five, and do things—go and 'blow up' farmhouses, and stuff like that. And they had troops looking for us, two thousand looking for eighty of us. They found one or two.

J: Really?! Out of—

M: Out of about ten days, out of about eighty of us. And we sat on the hilltops. And they didn't use helicopters or planes or anything. We sat on the hilltops and watched them. It was kind of like Boer War stuff, they would go up and down, searching for us in grid-like formations, and we'd just watch; and could see exactly what they were up to; and then we'd duck out and sort of hide away, and come out at night and go to a farmhouse and have a meal with the farmer, because they knew what was going on. And we'd say, "Now we've 'blown up' your house, and we're off. Please phone them and say that this has happened".

And we'd go. We'd send up a flare just as we left, to show that we'd blown it up, and we'd run. And, they didn't find us! And now I'm telling you all this because we were dressed in the overalls that the cleaning staff had to wear—

Young Spiegel at army training camp, 1967

J: As the terrorists?

M: We didn't have the regular uniform, the regular overalls that we normally had … We were told, "You can't use your regular uniform", [and] we were made to look different. But they didn't just find any something different. They found what they had, and what they had was what the black cleaners used. Interesting, eh?

J: Who was the enemy, exactly? Communism?

M: The enemy was … black people … But when I said to the staff sergeant—the guy who trained us on these radar things— because we were ten or more miles behind the front, and I remember saying to him, "Listen, why do we have to carry these bloody rifles around"? Because we were way behind what was happening, and if suddenly they started coming here, we'd just head off backwards. We'd always be behind the front. "So why do we need to carry these rifles?" And he looked at me and he said, "When the shit hits the fan, and the communists come over the hill, then it's every man for himself."

There's your answer; but the communists came in black skins for the most part. No—I'm wrong, he didn't say "the communists". He said, "The Russians come over the hill"! So it was the Russians. So they would have been white. But, actually, the enemy was black. Eh, it was messy. There was no enemy. That stuff hadn't really begun in 1967. It was only just beginning. The enemy was mostly the Russians, the Soviet Union ...

J: So the idea of the enemy was this big stuff happening in the world, but you were really fighting the cleaners, actually.

M: Right, or their brothers ...

So, to jump forward, after that camp in Potchefstroom in '69, I then used anthropology as an excuse to keep on going to Lesotho. And as I finished my honours [degree] in '75, they were going into Angola. And then they got serious. They really did want me. And I wasn't registered yet as a Master's student, so I didn't have an excuse.

I thought I was going to go. They wanted me for three weeks in December and I thought, "I can't get out of this". And then they changed their tune. They postponed it for a few weeks, and then said they were going to want me for three months. I'd gotten my research job with Philip Mayer in Grahamstown. I was in Jo'burg, because the research was based, at that point, in Soweto. As soon as [the army] changed it all, I got onto a plane—first time I ever did this—and flew out of Jo'burg on the first plane out to Port Elizabeth. I drove up to Grahamstown, registered as a student, came back, and I was home the same night; it was my wife's birthday—the 14th of January. The first birthday since we were married, we'd just gotten married ...

So I registered for the Master's. And also I got a letter [from Rhodes University in Grahamstown] saying that I was a key person in a research project funded by the Chamber of Mines, and that I couldn't be released for military service. And I managed to get out [of army service] again. And I never went back to the army. But, I mean, for years … I didn't answer the phone. At that point, my brother had a flat in Jo'burg, and he and his wife were away and my wife and I were living there … and … I didn't answer the front door. And it was *years*—I still don't use my name when I answer the phone.

If I answer the phone now I say "Hello". There was a time when I would just say the telephone number. And if it was anybody that didn't recognise my voice and said, "Can I speak to Andrew Spiegel"? —I wasn't always called Mugsy at that point—I would say, "Who's calling, I'll see if he's in". And if I could avoid answering it I would let my wife answer, and she wouldn't call me to the phone, but would find out who was there. And [answering] the front door [too] …

J: And what was the fear exactly …?

M: That they'd come—they did, they came round to the door to fetch you to go to the army. I knew it was happening, that it happened! The same friend, the chemist, he was also under the same threat, and he … he told me they had come around to his place, not far away. And one day, he came around to our house, to our flat, unannounced. My wife opened the door only when I was out of the back door, only when I was gone. And then eventually, when I saw it was clear, I came back to see what was going on, and she was in tears. I mean, it was just all the stress about this stuff. And I remember going to see another friend, whom I'd been close to here at UCT. Because by then I had become quite active politically, and he'd been involved too. I was at his parents' house in Jo'burg, trying to warn him about what was going on. He had Irish ancestry, and was busy getting himself an Irish passport to leave the country. I don't think he ever came back. I was in his parents' home and the military arrived. "Where is he"? they asked. His mother had to say, "I haven't seen him in months. Dunno. Gone". It was horrible stuff.

J: And they were sending them to Angola at this time? That's where everyone was going?

M: And I managed to get out of going to Angola. I thank Philip Mayer and that migrant labour project for that. The 'Black Villagers in an Industrial Society' stuff ... the stuff [I wrote] on the developmental cycle, I don't know if you've read that ... but what was interesting even then, I mean, I did the honours [degree]— which was on migrant labour—for which I was lucky. I was the only honours student. Before that, when I was in third year—no actually it was my second year—Martin West grabbed me and said, "you're interested in Lesotho, there's somebody who wants some work done in Lesotho, 1,000 dollars to do it", which was quite a lot of money in those days ... two transfers of 500 dollars. And "if you're interested in migrant labour—the effects of migrant labour on Christian marriage in Lesotho", that's what they wanted me to look at. So I was lucky. He knew I was heading to Lesotho every vacation, so it provided me with another justification for going, and on the basis of that I got the job with Philip Mayer on migrant labour.

That then allowed me to do a Master's degree, which I switched to when I came back to UCT later, and registered and completed it here. Which is actually part of the story you need to know. I'll come back to that. While I was finishing the Master's there was no apparent job on the horizon, and I was thinking of becoming a plumber ... of doing a plumber's training so I'd have a technical skill. And I came very close. And then Sally Frankental, who was a very junior member of the department at the time, was asked to help create the [Kaplan] Centre for Jewish Studies. So ... they needed a replacement for three years; and I got that job, and that kept me here. So it was still touch and go. I mean, I was completely taken by anthropology. But by now I had a wife and a child, and I actually had to have a job. I couldn't just keep on roaming.

Spiegel in Lesotho with South African Voluntary Service (SAVS)

Chapter 3

UCT in the '70s

"...it was all this kind of musical chairs. And it's important to relate that because the country's anthropology was very small ... and the boycott didn't help"

J: So you became an assistant lecturer?

M: No, a junior lecturer, which was a temporary position. [Sally Frankental] had a permanent appointment [in Social Anthropology], and I was a temporary junior lecturer for three years. But let's go back to "Why did I come back to UCT"? That's part of what you need to know.

In 1973, in my second year, Monica Wilson retired. I had done my first year in '72, went to her and said, "Please let me do the second year course and the 'additional' course together, because I want to make best use your presence while you're still here, because you'll be gone in '74". She allowed me to do that. She retired in '73, and in '74 they then advertised her job, but they didn't manage to make an appointment until they agreed to appoint somebody in '77 who started in '78, so there was a long hiatus.

At that point there was no such thing as an associate professor, or hardly. They had established chairs of a department, and the professor was the head of the department and the chair, and effectively was everything else too. And Monica had retired so they had to appoint someone called 'acting head of the department'. The department was pretty small. It was Monica, Michael Whisson, Martin West, and Sally, although it was extended by having another sub-department in it called Comparative African Government and Law (CAGL), which had grown out of the Native Administration section during the old colonial time. That section was pretty radical. It had been headed, for a while before I came, by Jack Simons, who was forced into exile after uh ... I think he was a member of the

Communist Party. His daughter taught when I was here. Mary Simons is now in Politic Studies and is due to retire very soon, either this year or next.

And there were two others. David Welsh was in the department. He might have been called an associate professor at that point, maybe not. The head of that [Social Anthropology and CAGL] department was an *acting* head for a while … when Monica retired and they advertised the job. A fellow called Joe Loudon, who was a South African who went abroad, applied for it but wasn't offered the job. I don't understand why. He was interviewed but wasn't offered the job. Another applicant who *was* offered the job was Joan Vincent, who then managed to secure herself a permanent full professorship at Columbia on the basis of this other offer. She did actually come here in '79 and spent a year as a visitor, which was great. It was a pity she didn't take the job, but Columbia is a hell of a lot more prestigious than Cape Town. Um, and … meanwhile Michael Whisson … applied and was turned down twice. I went to Rhodes around that time.

During 1975 when I did my Honours, Whisson and I fell out. I wasn't very much younger than these people, because I had spent time at Wits [before coming to UCT]. Martin West was *two* years older than I! Michael was maybe eight or nine years older than that, but no more … In some respects we were all pretty much of an age of … same as everybody.[1] Michael was probably the oldest, other than Monica, and followed by Sally who is six years older than I. Um … so, we were quite close in age, although there was something of an age gap between Whisson and me. From my perspective, he was not a nice man, and he and I fell out … Martin had been his student or was *mentored* but was never supervised by him. Monica had supervised Martin's stuff. Maybe Michael had supervised Martin's Honours. The two of them were quite close, but then they also fell out. So, somehow … things weren't working particularly well for me at that stage.

I took the job at Rhodes because there was nothing else [at UCT]. But I was quite happy to get out of UCT because UCT's

---

[1] Spiegel recently learned that Whisson is in fact twelve years his senior.

anthropology at that point wasn't a happy space. I did the [Rhodes] research and there was a Master's coming out of it, which was great … My Honours, I got a really bad mark for it—partly because I was jolling [partying] too much, doping too much, had just met my wife, so it wasn't uh … but also partly because Whisson and I didn't get on. Whisson had inherited an external examiner in the form of David Hammond-Tooke from Monica Wilson. Whisson and Hammond-Tooke didn't get on, but Whisson wasn't senior enough to be able to convince the institution to change external examiners, and because he was an *acting* head of department. The hierarchies were much stronger than they are now …

Hammond-Tooke didn't like the stuff which came out of this department, especially if Whisson had anything to do with it. Whisson actually had very little to do with my Honours dissertation—nothing; although he claimed to be my supervisor and then did nothing and left it all to me; and Martin West had kind of led me into it, so, there was tension between them about it. I had suddenly been taken over by Whisson when West had taken some interest in me to begin with, found me the [Honours research] job, originally, though neither gave me much guidance. And Hammond-Tooke came along and slated it … what had happened for a couple of years in between, since Monica had retired, is that Whisson would defend his students against Hammond-Tooke, and the mark would go up; but he didn't defend me, so I came out with a third [class pass] for my Honours. Which didn't help. So I couldn't have actually stayed here anyway, at that point.

The next few years go on, I go to Rhodes, I start doing the work, and clearly I've got, you know … a body of material for my Master's. There was no coursework Master's in those days, just dissertation only. Philip Mayer, whom I was working with, was getting old. At retirement, I think he was sixty-seven or sixty-eight, or something like that. And he had this research project, it was fully funded … he had no teaching responsibilities whatsoever, he was doing nothing for the [Rhodes University Anthropology] Department, he was nominally in the post. And I said to him one day:

27

Philip, why are you hanging onto this post? What's the point? Why do you wanna be there? Because you're never gonna go back to it. Your salary is paid for by this project—by the time this project is over you will be forced to retire, so you will never be able to go back to the department. And ... what's happening now is they are having to recruit temps in to do this stuff. So everything's in kind of limbo in the department. Just resign, but stay on as a full professor. You'll stay on senate, you'll stay on everything else, and your salary is paid ...

And he kind of looked at me as though to say: "What's this bloody student saying to me?!" But we got on quite well. He was a German Jew, and my father was a German Jew, um ... and he retired within a couple of weeks. And then what had been his job came up and was advertised.

Now, this was during the [academic] boycott days. By that point it was really difficult to find anybody to come here [as UCT's experience showed]. This was '77, early '77 ... might even be late '76. That's partly why they couldn't find anyone for Monica's job, because people wouldn't come. And it got worse, it got more intense as years went by. In the first round of applicants for the job at Rhodes, Martin West and a fellow called Allie Dubb were interviewed. Allie Dubb was at Wits. He was turned down, and from what I understood was told he wouldn't get the job ... I liked him, but he wasn't particularly good at what he did. Martin West was offered the job. He was a senior lecturer here [at UCT], and he was only too pleased to be getting away from Whisson ... He was offered the job, came back to Cape Town, and told the administration here that he had been offered the job at Rhodes. They said, "Can we see your CV please?" He'd never formally applied—from what I understand—for the professorship here [at UCT]. He was offered it ... At which point, Rhodes then re-advertised and then another Wits person applied, a guy called Gerard Schutte who was in anthropology at Wits. He was offered the job, and Wits then appointed him as professor of sociology. So once again Rhodes was left without anybody, advertised a third time, and this time Whisson applied and got it. Which was just as well because of the tensions in [UCTs] department at that point,

28

since Martin West was now going to be a professor and the head of department. Martin had leap-frogged over his own mentor ... and there was a lot of disruption and conflict between members of the UCT Anthropology—including CAGL—Department ...

When UCT appointed Martin, it suddenly left a whole lot of people on the wrong side. For example, Robin Palmer [then a lecturer at UCT] had taken a position to support the Whisson side of this. So, when Whisson went to Grahamstown and had another junior job to fill there, Robin went along and was offered it while John Sharp, having just completed his PhD at Cambridge, got a job here at UCT. It was all a kind of musical chairs. It's important to relate that, because the country's anthropology was very small. As illustration, I was the only UCT Honours student in my year. Two years before me, I think there were three: Pat McAllister, Alex Petersen, and another fellow whose name I've forgotten. Pat went on to become an anthropologist at Rhodes. Alex Petersen didn't continue ... and the other person also didn't. The year before me there was just one guy, and he went on into industry. So it was pretty thin. At Wits too, the year before me, there were three Honours students I think. And one of *them* went into industry and got his PhD eventually—Kent McNamara, who worked in the Chamber of Mines in Human Resources his whole life. Another, Martin Peskin, left academia and went abroad, and again, the third, I don't even know what happened to him—but there were relatively few. Also, those who did make it often left the country ... Joao de Pina Cabral, I knew him then too. He might have been in Honours during the same year as I was, but at Wits. He went abroad and he's now a professor of anthropology in Portugal, a leading figure there and subsequently in the European Association of Social Anthropologists (EASA).[2] But there were very few, and among those that there were, many also fled the country, most did ... and there were not many newcomers coming in. So it was a very small little circle of people, and the [academic] boycott didn't help.

---

[2] He has since moved to the United Kingdom.

M: Here again is a bit of earlier history ... Radcliffe-Brown founded this department. He was succeeded by a man called T.T. Barnard, whom nobody knows much about other than that he used to be up here [in the Arts Block building], and had a *heliograph*—a sort of mirror thing—which he shone down to his wife at home somewhere down in Rondebosch to say "I'm coming home, get supper ready", or lunch ready, or whatever ... This is the story, anyway. And he was particularly interested in Kirstenbosch. He wasn't much of an anthropologist. And then he left and Isaac Schapera came [before leaving for the UK]. Then Monica Wilson came. She [had taught at Rhodes University] for some years. She reportedly left to come [to UCT] simply because, at that stage she was a widow, she had two children and ... there was gender discrimination at Rhodes. She was a full professor but, because she was a woman, she earned less than a man did in the same position. The idea was that women should be supported by men earning the main salary ... UCT didn't have that principle.

Monica came here [to UCT]. She would, I believe, much rather have stayed in Grahamstown. Her family home was in Hogsback [not far from Grahamstown]. She ended up being here for 20 years. But she left Rhodes for that [gender discrimination] reason. Astonishing stuff isn't it? In '53, she came here ... and I think that's when Philip Mayer started at Rhodes! I think that's right. I don't think there was anybody in between there. And [Mayer], interestingly—a lawyer by first training in Germany—had to sit his final oral exam in moot, in private, because the Nazi youth wouldn't let Jews do this any longer. He then went into exile. His father was a professor and a social historian who wrote what people said was the definitive biography of Engels. He'd gone to Oxford. Philip followed him, and was hanging around Oxford. Philip ... decided there was nothing for him there, and he went to Palestine—this was before the [the second world] war—to work with the Zionist

30

movement. And, because he was a lawyer, he was being used to work on negotiations to buy land from Palestinian residents to set up things like the Kibbutzim and stuff, for the Jewish agency and ... as he later explained, he decided he needed to know more about these people, because he didn't understand them. He went back to Oxford to find out where he could study ... He ended up with an Egyptologist to begin with, who said, "No, no, you don't want to talk to us, you must find this man called Radcliffe-Brown". So he kind of ended up with Radcliffe-Brown, and then, went off to what was then called Persia and did a PhD there ... I'm not sure what it was about, I'd need to look it all up. Um, and then, when he was just kind of also unemployed, he somehow bumped into Radcliffe-Brown, on a bus in London I think, and Radcliffe-Brown said, "There's a job going in South Africa". Mayer [had found] a job for a while, as a government ethnologist in Kenya, and then he went back [to Britain] and that's when he ran into Radcliffe-Brown and ended up in Grahamstown as a professor there—knowing nothing much about South Africa at all.

He stayed there [at Rhodes] for a while and then got itchy feet, and wanted to move up in the world. Grahamstown wasn't good enough for him, and he took the job at Wits at some point—I don't know the chronology of the Wits professorships ... He stayed there for a couple of years. He and his wife hated Jo'burg ... Philip Mayer then went to Bradford in England for three or four years. Hammond-Tooke, who had been a South African government ethnologist but then became professor at Rhodes, then left Rhodes University and went to Wits, and the Rhodes job was vacant and Mayer went back to Rhodes ... full circle—where he lived quite happily for the rest of his career. But do you see the point: these small little circles of people ...!

It was a very small circle. They all knew each other. The world's anthropologists—certainly the British world's anthropologists, which were at the British colonial [universities]—they all knew each other! They were all uh ... were either friends or hated each other, but they knew each other. It was a very small world, none of the kind of thousands of members of the 'triple-A' [the American Anthropological Association]. They didn't necessarily *see* each other

31

that often, because travel wasn't that easy; so communication was by letters which took two weeks on the boats to get across to the other place. But they knew each other pretty well, it was small, and here in South Africa it was particularly so.

Um ... so there's a bit of history, so that's Philip Mayer and me. And why did I come back to UCT? Because when Whisson went to Rhodes in '78 I left, because I wasn't going to be in a department with Whisson. I had contacted Martin West and said, "Look, uh, you're coming into this new job, I've got this work that I've done, I'd like to switch my registration back to UCT. Are you able to take me on?" He, starting a new department, needed every body he could find, especially graduate students. He'd lost the whole department. I mean, Whisson had gone, Palmer had gone, Sharp was new, Sally Frankental was here—she was here for quite a bit of time. At that point she was a junior lecturer, which was also a tenure track job ... When I had that post, it wasn't any longer. And so [Martin West] started with, basically, himself and Sally: a professor and junior lecturer. Sharp was a temporary person appointed to a lectureship, he'd just got his PhD. [West] had to build the place up, so of course, he pulled in every potential person he could. And so I came back in the middle of '78. And then within a year, by the time I'd finished the Master's—while I was worrying about what job I'd find and considered training as a plumber—the possibility of a job came up, of doing Sally's job. But you see again how *small* ...?!

And there wasn't any likelihood of [West] finding anybody else to come, to pull in easily, who would stay for a long time. There'd be short-term visitors. Colin Murray had come for a year as he prepared for his PhD. He had his first degree from Cambridge ... then gone the PhD process. His supervisor there would have been, I think, Meyer Fortes, who again, another South African, was a friend of Monica. Monica was a kind of local supervisor. And [Colin] came here and spent a year learning Sesotho, finding his way around, and taught for a while, for that year.

He was here in the middle of my first undergraduate year to the middle of my second year and beat me to winning the heart of a woman in my class whom I fancied ... And we became quite good friends, Colin and I. He used to lecture me, first year—on kinship—in the Beattie Theatre, and then we'd walked off together to a Sotho class where we were students together. He was just a year older than I.

So Colin was here for a bit. Alan Barnard too, whom you might have heard of, he was also here ... a year after, he came in the middle of the following year ...'73, just prior to Monica's retirement. Alan is a very shy fellow ... Emile Boonzaier will tell you about Alan Barnard's first ever tutorial, because Emile was a student in it. Alan came in—at that stage you were allowed to smoke in classrooms—he came in smoking his pipe. He waited for somebody to say something; everybody waited for the tutor to say something. Nobody said anything. After twenty minutes he got up and left. That's how shy he was. He's not so shy any more. He's a funny fellow. He worked with the Bushmen. We always wondered how he ever talked to anybody.

And then a guy named Rick Huntington also came, at the same time as Barnard. He was an American who had worked in Madagascar. Alan Barnard was here because he really was enamored with Radcliffe-Brown, he wanted to be in Radcliffe-Brown's space, and then went off and did his fieldwork in Botswana on the Bushmen and has since written theory, a 'Histories of Theory' textbook, because he had always had this fascination with Radcliffe-Brown. And uh ... Rick Huntington came because there was some money available for a temporary lecturer. It was because Monica's job was coming vacant, so there was free money. And so these visitors came. Rick was finishing a PhD, was writing up his PhD, which was a structuralist analysis of his work in Madagascar; and he also taught in the department. And it was the first real structuralist analysis that was introduced here—Levi Straussian stuff. Whisson had tried to teach that stuff, but pretty boringly, and failed, at least as I saw it. Huntington did a pretty great job of it.

J: What kind of theory was the focus of the department during this time?

M: It was almost all structural-functionalism. Monica didn't ever see beyond it. She saw history, she sort of liked the idea of history, but it was a very structured and—a structural-functionalist type of history. You may have read her chapters in *The Oxford History of South Africa*. That was the kind of—that was what she did as her final work, plus her *Religion and the Transformation of Society* book, which was an attempt to kind of re-look at her earlier stuff—before 1945—that she had done with Godfrey [her late husband]. And also social change, but it never really moved much further than what she'd done then in the late 1940s. And I *think* she watered down Godfrey Wilson's more radical position. I think that, but I've never been able to prove it.

It was whole-year courses at that time [not just semesters]. In first year, you did structural-functionalism. You did a section on kinship, a section on politics, a section on religion, and a section on economics. Maybe a little touch on socialisation somewhere, a bit of cultural relativism, and ... race—race and racism. Race, really. What is race, and what are the problems of race. And each student, by the end of the year, had to have read at least one of the old South African monographs. Also, for every essay you had to write drawing on ethnographic material from the monograph you had chosen. And it was Monica's book [*Reaction to Conquest*], it was Eileen Krige's *The Realm of a Rain-Queen*, it was Schapera's book on the Tswana ... um, and Hammond-Tooke's on *Bhaca Society*, I think was amongst them. The Kriges' Zulu one they didn't like because it wasn't first hand research. Monica didn't allowed Ashton's *The Basuto* because, I think, she didn't like Hugh Ashton who had written that one and then gone off to become a museum person in Bulawayo—and whose son is now a psychiatrist here in Cape Town, Paul Ashton. Um ... I don't remember what else in the way of recommended local ethnographic monographs. So that was how it was run. The second year was ... more of the same really. ... And looking at symbolism sort of in more and more detail—and, again, same principle—you had to choose one ethnographic monograph. But

34

they all had to be African ... Audrey Richards *Land, Labour, and Diet in Northern Rhodesia, The Nuer,* by Evans-Pritchard, the Tallensi ones by Meyer Fortes, and there was Evans-Pritchard's *Witchcraft, Oracles and Magic among the Azande.*

So ... it was that set of kind of classical, uh, structural-functionalist monographs. There was a bit of structuralism taught in the second year. I was taught by Rick Huntington. He taught his own stuff and he did it really well. He took his own stuff from Madagascar and taught around that, so we really learnt the principles from applying them. But that was as far as we got, there was nothing else. There wasn't even talk, until Robin Palmer arrived, of transactionalism, which by that time was really quite big and quite strong in Britain ... It was taking the formalist economic anthropology idea and saying, actually, you can take this into human social interaction. So it was sort of saying "I wouldn't waste my time talking to you now unless there were something I was going to gain from it"; that kind of stuff. So, it wasn't just material transaction, it wasn't just goods and services. It was service taken to its greatest extreme; that there's no interaction without both parties in it aiming to gain something from it. And that became quite big. It was followed by symbolic interactionism, but I don't remember that being taught to us.

... Fredrik Barth and Boissevain, Freddie Bailey, they were doing transactionalism and, most of them ... in Britain, were applying this stuff around the Mediterranean. The stuff on honour and shame came out of that ... it's the same kind of broad principles as one finds in symbolic interactionism, although symbolic interaction goes further because it actually talks about dialectical relationships. But it was basically sort of a walking away from the structural stuff of .... because everything was so neatly boxed [with structural-functionalism], and it was quite clear that things weren't so neatly boxed in reality. And people who worked in the Mediterranean were saying. "Well you can't—which are these societies? Where are their boundaries?" And so it was the beginning of [addressing the] problems of ethnicity; but it also moved away from big structuralist analysis to a focus on individuals, which transactionalism went into. It presumed that all of society was driven by individuals; and that culture was understood to grow out of individual interactions too—so that principles and rules grew out of interactions rather than the rules just dominating people. But the dialectical stuff wasn't there yet.

So it was the obverse of the old structuralists—the structuralism of structural-functionalism, not the structuralism of Levi-Strauss. That was very deep. It was such deep structure it didn't matter where it came from. But that [transactionalism] only came [to UCT] a little later, when Robin Palmer arrived …

***

"…he had the Wits copy, the only one in the country at the time"

And then, in '75 when I did Honours, there was the beginning of a shift … Hammond-Tooke had a funny department at Wits. He'd employed a geographer called Jeremy Keenan who wanted to be up at the forefront of everything; and he had discovered some of the Marxist anthropology stuff that was coming into vogue then. The sort of stuff which came in after Poulantzas, in anthropology, people like Meillassoux, Claude Meillassoux … Maurice Godelier, whom Sahlins had also discovered. And [Keenan] taught some of that. And because, again, they had a vacant job at UCT—the professorship was still not filled—they brought down both him and David Webster from Wits to be guest lecturers at UCT. David had gone another direction; he'd gone into componental analysis of kinship terminology, real structuralist stuff, very boring, I thought. Hammond-Tooke pushed him in that direction.

[David] came to teach us that and I remember thinking—I didn't know David at that point—"Why do I wanna learn this crap? It's completely irrelevant to anything, to life out there!" But … there was a whole corpus of it that came out, particularly out of the States. Out of the Chomskian … in a way, out of his structural linguistics. And little did I know that David was actually sort of

36

heading down the Marxist line rapidly. He came to teach us this kinship stuff and I got pissed off. And Jeremy Keenan came down for three or four weeks, and he taught the Meillassoux and Godelier stuff. I remember sitting with him in that Honours class where I was the only Honours student but marking first-year essays in vast numbers ... I was the only Honours student, so put into a class with a number of 'additional' course students ... I was attached to them as the kind of senior student, the monitor—that was my Honours. So it didn't make being an Honours student particularly easy. I was always way ahead of them, so there was no challenge. Which was probably also why I came out with such a bad mark because I didn't push myself.

I remember sitting in the class with Jeremy Keenan who was teaching us about social reproduction, from Meillassoux. It was the first time this notion had ever come to any of us. And we were reading this piece in which he talked about social reproduction, a piece called 'From Production to Reproduction'. And we were struggling with it. And Jeremy couldn't explain. And we kept saying, "What does this really mean? What's reproduction? I mean reproduction is about people having sex and producing babies. I mean, what are you talking about!? Explain". And he couldn't, because he didn't actually understand either. And eventually he said, 'look, I think the problem is that Meillassoux writes in French and ... *reproduction* in French means something different' ... and that was his explanation, along with a wave of his hands in a rolling motion! So it took me a couple of years to discover what it really meant. Jeremy also taught us from Godelier. *Rationality and Irrationality [in Economics]*, a really interesting book, published I think in '74 or '75. So it was a brand new thing, he had the Wits copy, the only one in the country at the time.

[Keenan] taught the second year [students] from it and he taught it to us in the honours/'additional' class too. And I went to all the second year classes because I wanted to learn this stuff. And at the end of it all I said, "Do you mind if I borrow the book for the few days before you go back to Jo'burg?" He'd been reading directly from the book, to the classes. So ... we didn't get taught very much we just got read the bloody story, and I could have read it myself ... So that was '75—this was the beginning for me of the Marxist stuff.

[In] '72, when I arrived [at UCT], Wolpe had published his piece, which would have given us some inkling, but nobody pointed us to it. I was pointed [to it] by one of the radicals at the campus at the time, Mike Morris, who now runs the CSSR [The Centre for Social Science Research]. Mike Morris, not Michael, because there was a security policeman called Michael Morris and Mike wanted to distinguish himself ... [Mike Morris] was an economist, or economic historian, who became a really radical, hard-line structuralist-Marxist for a while. Mike introduced me to Andre Gunder Frank; but this wasn't in anthropology. So I bought the Andre Gunder Frank's books and was reading that stuff in '73, I think, before anybody here [in anthropology at UCT] was talking dependency theory or anything like that. I was kind of finding my way into that stuff in a very haphazard fashion. I'd also read a bit of Eric Fromm about Marx when I was at Wits, in an extra-mural course.

So—finding my way—I was the first person here, in this department [at UCT], to really work with that stuff. My Honours dissertation wasn't good because I didn't really understand what I was writing about. I was trying to apply it. And of course Hammond-Tooke and Whisson would have hated it because both of them were rabidly anti-Marxist, all the way. If you read Hammond-Tooke's book, [*Imperfect Interpreters* (1997)], about South African anthropology, his history of—he has a go at me for my Marxism ... I actually pushed it harder, at that point in my analyses, than David Webster managed to ... As David got into politics directly, I was trying to bring it into the classroom and into the discipline much more. I've [critiqued] Hammond-Tooke along the way as well. I hammered him at one point about his going into Levi-Straussian structuralism and just disappearing from sight— forgetting about the political economy of the country. I've hammered his approach because I also think it closed off cultures, which I think was dangerous. It just simply fed into what the apartheid ideologues wanted.

Also, I then, through a student, Julia Segar, discovered something that I still have to take Hammond-Tooke on trust about.

In '84 I think, '83 or '84 ... Julia was one of our students at the time who had been working where I was working, in Matatiele in the then-Transkei. She had been reading Hammond-Tooke's book on chieftainship in the Transkei, *Command or Consensus*. This was from when [Hammond-Tooke] was still doing something which had political relevance. Julia then went to the Carnegie conference on poverty here in '84. There was a paper presented by three people from the University of Transkei, and they had lifted almost word for word from Hammond-Tooke's *Command or Consensus* for a large chunk of their paper in order to talk about chieftainship. In the process of looking up the stuff for herself, [Julia then] went and looked at another earlier text than *Command or Consensus,* one written by ... an American-based political scientist who had worked in South Africa, [Gwendolen Carter, *The Politics of Inequality*]. And Julia came back and said, "Mugsy ... same text in both" ...—and Hammond-Tooke's stuff [*Command or Consensus*] had come out later.

And I actually confronted [Hammond-Tooke] about it. I said, "David, how did this happen? What's going on here?" He said, "Mugsy, you've got to place this in time. I was working with Gwendolen Carter, I was doing a whole lot of that fieldwork, I wrote that, but she couldn't acknowledge me as the author—I actually wrote that stuff". And I've got to take that on faith. Unless sometime I find Gwendolen Carter's archives and find his texts sent to her, and find out if that archive confirms that that was the case. I've never tried to follow it up. But ... asking that question of this man who was old enough to be my father, who was the professor, who'd been my [Honours research essay] external examiner ...

When I went to [occupy an office at] Wits, as was starting the research job with Rhodes, I went to him. I said, "Professor Hammond-Tooke, you gave me this third class [mark]. I'm not fighting about the mark. It's behind us. I want to know what's wrong with this piece of work so I don't do it again". He struggled to tell me. He realised he couldn't justify it, because what had happened is he had put it down and Whisson hadn't defended it. So he was stuck, and I was stuck with the mark that it came with.

J: How much long after ...?

M: Only a few—two months! I submitted that in November of 1975 and I started working in Jo'burg in ... late December 1975. And I was up there just between Christmas and New Year and started working. I had an office on the Wits campus, with Allie Dubb, actually—see how small it is!?—at the Centre for African Studies, or the Institute for African Studies, as they called it at the time. And a month or so later, there I was having words with Hammond-Tooke ... There's always been a kind of ... since then, it's not been a happy relationship. He was also good to me. There was something I wrote once for a conference paper in '85 or '86. He was at the conference, and it was a kind of dry run for a conference I was going to in Britain a couple of months later. And he said, "Mugsy, I want that paper"—he was the editor of *African Studies* at the time—"I want that paper for *African Studies*" ... But there was a book due to come out of the UK conference. I eventually kind of gave it to him and wrote it in a different format for the book. So it wasn't all bad. And in the last few years [that we had contact] we were sort of friendly to one another.

Similarly, Whisson and I will see each other and there will be civility. But, I mean, he's the kind of guy who will always find a way to make some cutting remark ... whatever the context. So I'm civil to him, anticipating something nasty or biting's going to come, and I don't rise to the bait any longer. That's the only difference. Because there's no point ... He's retired in Grahamstown. I think he's a city councillor, a DA (Democratic Alliance) city councillor, and a lay-preacher in the Grahamstown cathedral. He's an interesting fellow. Someday the Rhodes bunch should actually write something about him. It's interesting they haven't ... because he was there for quite a long time, from '78 ... Martin [West] returned from [a year in] America, became the professor here [at UCT], Whisson got into his car and drove to Grahamstown, and I drove from Grahamstown back [to UCT].

J: [Laughs, makes hand gestures indicating two travelers passing each other when heading in opposite directions]

M: No not that way around because we drive on the other side of the road! [Laughs]. And, I always sort of joke that as we passed each other on the road we carefully looked the other way! [Laughs].

"'You mean social change, don't you?'"

M: Okay, back to … that 'additional' course in anthropology in my second year. I went to Monica and I said, "I want to do this". She said, "Well … what do you want to do in it?" I said, "I'd like to do something on development". She said, "You mean social change, don't you?" Interesting. She didn't like the idea of trying to cause change. So we did a whole chunk of stuff on social change. There were three of us in the class.

J: So by that time, did you have yet an idea of what you meant by development?

M: No; that was why I wanted to learn about it. And she then tried to disabuse me of the idea. Um, there were three of us. There was a woman from Namibia called Ursula Dentlinger who was interested in the Nama. I was interested in development and the Basotho. And the third was a fellow who was really bright and should've stayed in academia, but he was coloured and a political activist and that was a problem, called Brendon … Brendon Roberts, I think. I've bumped into him occasionally, since. And he … was fascinated by the Rwandan problem, which was blowing up already then. The genocide now, or relatively recently, was major, but it was already being written about by Maquet and others … Brendon was fascinated with all of that. So, [Monica] designed the first half of the year around social change and our respective areas … and then I think she handed us onto Rick Huntington to look after us, to do something else. Yes, and he taught—at least for

41

some part of it—the whole lot of Erik Erikson's *Childhood and Society*, and all the related socialisation stuff, and psychological anthropology, which nobody was doing here.

***

"Which freaked me out, because I suddenly couldn't write how terrible it was ... All I could say was, 'migrant labour is incorporated into people's lives'

...

...and history then became crucial"

M: ... What drove me to Lesotho to do my first bit of work, other than the opportunity, was to show how migrant labour was so negatively affecting people's lives in the rural areas—something that many others were saying. Men were being separated from their wives and their children for long periods of time; children were being brought up without men as role models, without men around, without fathers around; and women were kind of at their wits end having to do all of this ... And I heard from people ... one women—and I've told you this bit before—said to me, "But we've always done it this way, as long as I can remember". I've told you that part hey?

J: I don't think so.

M: Haven't I? Okay. In Lesotho; 1973: up on a hill, a woman comes to me—behind the village—and she says, "What exactly are you actually doing here?" I said, "Well, the project is—I've been asked to look at the effects of migrant labour on Christian marriage in Lesotho". I said, "But since you are all Christian, it's effects generally on marriage in Lesotho as far as I'm concerned". And she looked at me for a moment and she said, "That's really a stupid question, because my grandfather and my father and uncles, and my brothers and husband, and my sons and now my grandsons have been or are all migrant labourers. That's how we live" ... Basically she was saying "we've adapted"— though she didn't use those words—"we've adapted to life with men away, and that's how our life works". The effects? Well there are no control groups. She was saying—again she didn't use these words of course—"Who are you gonna compare us with?" Because,—and this is throughout this country—"That's the way we live". Which freaked me out, because I suddenly couldn't write how terrible it was. Because she was saying "that's normal for us". So I had to then say, "Well, how do I then say what's normal for them is bad?" because I'd be critiquing their way of living—a direct contradiction of the kind of cultural relativism that came with the structural functionalism that I'd been taught.

So that took me to the Marxist stuff ... to get beyond the narrow confines of the village and those people themselves, to say, "Look, they've been hegemonised"—I didn't use that word, that was prior to Gramsci becoming significant in my world. "They've been ...co-opted into a system which is actually problematic. And they have ... false consciousness"—if you wish—"and so I need to show how the structures work which force them into a situation where they're all accepting this as normal", instead of trying to say how bad it was for them because they decried it—which they didn't! I now had to show *why* they were not decrying it. But doing that required a major shift for me.

J: Were you reading Marx at that time? What clued you in that Marxism is where you can talk about this?

M: I wasn't. When I was in the field doing that [research in 1973], I wasn't. When I came back from the field and I did in my Honours year, read Meillassoux and Godelier. That was '75; and, although much of the literature informing it was banned, there was a kind of new, neo-Marxist presence around. Harold Wolpe had written his now famous piece that was published in '72. That kind of made its way into circulation here, slowly, because you couldn't buy it, because anything that he wrote was banned .... And [the work of] Andre Gunder Frank, I'd been introduced to just before that. But I didn't fully understand it, none of us really understood this stuff ... we were grappling with it.

43

I came back [from the field] and what happened was, I wrote a first report which didn't bring any Marx into it; and then I read the Meillassoux stuff and I tried to apply it, um … not very well. That was my Honours dissertation, which, as I've said, I got a really bad mark for. So clearly, I didn't really understand it.

But I began to … and then I started fiddling further with it, and then I did further research in Lesotho for my Master's and … I struggled to write it—to write up my data. I came home to Rhodes at the time with masses of data, and didn't know how to begin to write—I couldn't think of an argument. All I could say was, " Migrant labour is incorporated into people's lives".

That project [the Migrant Labour Project under Philip Mayer] was funded by The Chamber of Mines. There was still an idea around when I went to the field mid 1976 that people worked in the mines to earn some extra money so they could come back home and buy … a new bicycle, or a new Hi-Fi set, or something like that … but that [a migrant labour wage] wasn't core to their existence. And I said, "Well, this just is not true". I'd been in Lesotho previously, and seen that; and now I went off to go and demonstrate, again, for my Master's that this was … that the money [they earned] was a central feature in everybody's lives, the remittances. That was how they lived. The [agricultural] fields that they worked were secondary. I soon came to show [as did Colin Murray around the same time] that they were even less than secondary. They depended on that migrant income, remittances, and they often didn't produce very much; that often it actually would have been better to have just kept the money and spent it on buying food than to invest in their fields. I wanted to sort of unpack all of that stuff, but I couldn't think how.

And I then read a whole lot of the Marxist stuff, and realised it was wrong, in the sense that the situation was so neatly understood, much of it simply in terms of class. There was a piece written about the Transkei [by Innes and O'Meara. It stated that,] people in the Transkei, those who were dispossessed of land, who had no land, were lumpenproletariat. They couldn't necessarily find jobs, and so they were a lumpenproletariat. The others, who were working in the cities, sending money home, were a proletariat. Others were working the fields and they were peasants. And I looked at this and thought, yes there are all those kind of categories of people in Lesotho where I've been. But when I look at who are the ones working and sending money home, they're mostly younger men. And part of what they're doing with their money is buying livestock and buying their way into having fields later. So they're actually building up a home so that when they retire, they'll look like peasants, but they aren't peasants. They've used their income to become peasant-like. Which is completely the reverse, of course, of the Marxian model.

I'd also been introduced, probably by Jeremy Keenan, to [Alexander] Chayanov in my Honours year—and his comments about the peasantry in Russia, pre-revolution: about how they sometimes did go out and work when … when the sort of primary couple of the household was on its own, they worked their fields, fed themselves, and then they got children and they had to increase their labour expenditure—their use of land—in order to feed their children. As their children got older and there were more children, then they increased their use more because they had more labour-power available and more mouths to feed. As the children peeled off and set out on their own, so they shrank their productivity, since they didn't need to feed so many people. They didn't keep on producing simply to accumulate for inheritance purposes, or supposedly to look after themselves in their old age. They just shrank what they used. So that whole cyclical thing which [Chayanov] presents, I was aware of it; and then I discovered— which I should have been taught but hadn't—that Meyer Fortes had written something similar, but in a different way, which he called *The Developmental Cycle of Domestic Groups*. Um, [in an edited volume], I think. And so then there was a bunch of articles around the same theme, from West Africa, where they looked at households and discovered a sort of growth and shrinkage with the family cycle.

So I put the two together, the Marxian stuff with that and said of the rural Lesotho population, "Actually, they're all a proletariat!" And I'll stick by that, to this day. If they're gonna use that kind of analysis, all of South Africa was proletarian—southern Africa had been proletarianised by the '50s at the very latest. Yes, there were people living a peasant-type existence, but almost none of them was able to do that without having first invested their earnings in proletarian or other wage-labour. So, the whole thing was interconnected; and that was my argument, but I struggled to get there, I really did. And I was able then to say, look, it's all one political economy and why those people are out there suffering is because of the greediness of the capitalists here in Johannesburg ... or in the Free State mines. And so I was able to get around that problem I'd faced on the hillside in Lesotho. Yes, they'd adapted! But it wasn't an adaptation of their own volition. It was an adaptation forced on them under circumstances not of their own making. And history then became crucial.

J: I've heard the comment that UCT, or that this department, was strictly Marxist for a long time.

M: Strictly Marxist, it never was. It was certainly the most Marxist-oriented department in the country, probably in the sub-continent, from the late 1970s—1979. Sharp was one of the examiners of my Master's dissertation. He'd come out of Cambridge with a transactionalist analysis, having produced a PhD thesis which was regarded as one of the best that Cambridge had ever seen. Sadly, it was never published. John ... tried to rework it into a Marxist analysis, which he could never fully do, so that's partly why it never got to the way he wanted it to do, wanted to make it—why it never got published. And we sort of swung into a much more Marxian analysis then. Colin Murray visited a couple of times, pushed it with us as well. And, all of them—I mean, I'd been taught it by someone at Wits, but the Wits department, at that point, didn't do much fieldwork. Jeremy Keenan, who taught it to me, the Marxian stuff ... I dunno, there was no ... ethnography going on. He wasn't South African, he'd never done South African fieldwork—he started out as a social geographer amongst the Tuareg. So that was part of the difficulty. And he did go back up to working in the desert with the Tuareg again, but he didn't have a South African interest. The other one who did do it, but didn't do it until later—and was also doing, or at least publishing, relatively little fieldwork at that point—was David Webster, also at Wits. David Hammond-Tooke, who objected to anything Marxist, wouldn't let it dominate that department.

Martin West, here [at UCT] let it dominate. Martin was never a Marxist, but he kind of accepted it and, taking a position that supported some eclecticism, let its influence grow, but alongside other approaches. That's why Robert Thornton was here, Robert was adamantly anti-Marxist. But we ran our seminars in the next door room [to where we are now in this interview] which used to be the tea-room. It used to be intensely … I mean … we used to knock each other about really hard. It was a frightening space to be in. But for the most part we came out of it as friends, even though we really went for each other whilst in there. But it was a really exciting learning space … we honed stuff together, and we taught it. John and I dominated it, I suppose. And then Caroline White was brought in [1982; with a Sussex PhD], and she also pushed [a Marxist perspective] very hard.

Spiegel (sitting front with blanket) at UCT student protest, 1973 at St. George's Cathedral in Cape Town. © Copyright Cape Times, Independent Newspapers

Chapter 4

Volkekunde and Academic Apartheid

"I was busy just finishing ... I think what was the first Marxist anthropology in this country as a Master's thesis in '79"

J: *...How did the politics of the time—*

M: The national politics?

J: *Especially in the mid to late '70s ... how did anthropologists—at UCT and elsewhere—react? Or how did they get involved?*

M: Well, first you've got to make the distinction between anthropologists at the Afrikaans-language universities and those at the English-language universities, which is a bit too crude, but it's an important start. In fact there were three kinds of universities in this country: the English-language universities; Afrikaans—I'm not sure why in this order—Afrikaans-language universities; and then what were known as 'bush colleges', which were places set up specifically for black students in their respective ethnic cohorts. UCT is the oldest, Stellenbosch is the second oldest, as far as I know, in the country. UNISA probably comes next ... I'm not sure when exactly it was established. UCT and Stellenbosch both had anthropology departments by that time (the apartheid years post-1948), but UCT's department, with Monica Wilson, was a liberal space. By the end of the early '80s it became increasingly ... slightly Marxist-liberal.

The anthropology department at Stellenbosch remained, until after the fall of apartheid, a *volkekunde* [or 'ethnos-theory'] department. The department had been founded by W.W.M. Eiselen, who became the secretary of Native Affairs under Verwoerd, who was, prior to becoming the Prime Minister who

49

took South Africa out of the British Commonwealth, the Minister of Native Affairs ... which tells you that they were real, down-the-line, ethnos theory pro-apartheid people. So that was here [the Western Cape]. I don't know the kind of history of all these universities, but by that stage—we'll sort of move around the coast—UWC (University of Western Cape) would have been founded sometime in the '60s, I think, as a university for coloured students. It wasn't intended for black students, it was intended for coloured students—'black' versus 'coloured' in the old apartheid categorisations. A whole lot of people came out of Afrikaans-language universities and taught in those bush colleges. There was a university set up in Port Elizabeth, also around that time. It was meant to be a dual-medium university, Afrikaans and English together, for whites. But because [English-language] Rhodes University, in Grahamstown, was older ... and there was some sense that it was another liberal establishment, the [apartheid regime, along with ethnos theorists felt they] had to have their own place in the Eastern Cape. So while the University of Port Elizabeth was dual-medium, the anthropology that was there was *volkekunde*.

J: When did volkekunde become ... kind of its own institution?

M: Early; from the start! The anthropology department in Stellenbosch was established as an anthropology department working with ethnos theory, which came out of Germany. John Sharp, in *the Journal of Southern African Studies* [in 1981], does something of a history of it, of the split, but particularly about *volkekunde* and when it starts in this country. Ideas which were being used in certain kinds of anthropology in Germany, pre-Second World War, in the hands of a man called Wilhelm Mühlmann, were brought to this country around that sort of time. They remained sort of peripheral in Germany for quite a long time, and Mühlmann remained in the academy long after the Second World War. [Ethnos theorists] became much more strident here than they were there. And they also built on a Russian fellow's work, a guy called

Shirokogoroff, but I don't remember the details, Sharp's piece would give you that.

J: Did UCT's department ever do volkekunde?

M: No, UCT never had that. UCT's anthropology department was started by Radcliffe-Brown, who saw anthropology as the sociology of 'primitive people'. And in a way, that's one of our battles here: that the sociologists say, "Well if that was how you started, now that there's no such notion as 'primitive people', then why should there be a separate department?" Which is a difficult [idea] to battle with, other than to say, "Well, you guys do something quite different from what we do". That battle is actually getting played out very soon again. Not only here, but in India—an Indian association [is attempting] to join the World Council of Anthropological Associations (WCAA). There are two anthropology associations in India anyway, and now this other one is a sociology association—that's what they call themselves. So it's kind of ... it's messy stuff.

...Okay, but ... let's go back. Rhodes [University's Anthropology Department] was also established by Radcliffe-Brown, quite a bit later ... So there was the same kind of [structural-functionalist, sociological] impetus there. Port Elizabeth, by the '70s, was a *volkekunde* department and Rhodes was a social anthropology department. Further up the coast, in Durban—the University of Natal, as it was known—had a social anthropology focus. Even further up the coast, or just outside, there was the University of Durban-Westville, created in the '60s. It didn't exist before that. It was designed explicitly for Indians, just like UWC [was for coloureds]. And it was ... also kind of *volkekunde* ... like UWC, it was kind of a hybrid. They were trying not to be straight *volkekunde*, some of them, but they, variously amongst them, couldn't see their way out of it. They'd come out of the *volkekunde* tradition, most of them were taught there, but they tried to do kind of a balancing act. UNISA also tried that ... I'll come back to them when I get around—I'll keep going geographically.

51

Further north was the University of Zululand ... So one for coloureds, one for Indians, one for Zulus ... Oh there was—I forgot—the University of Transkei ... uh, and Fort Hare, I've left those out. That's an interesting slip that I've left those out as we move along. The University of Fort Hare is an older institution, which had been a sort of subsidiary of Rhodes at one point. And then it kind of was turned into another 'bush college', having been re-designed, ostensibly for the Xhosa. But because the Xhosa were split between the Ciskei and the Transkei—and that's sort of political, sort of local-level politics stuff—when the Transkei was established, it was being, sort of, imagined as a separate Bantustan. The University of Transkei was also then created. So there were two Xhosa universities. And in part, that was also because Fort Hare had a bit more of a liberal history. The University of Transkei was also ... I mean—you saw a fellow from the Transkei [Masilo Lamla] at the [recent ASnA—2011] conference. He's still a product of that old stuff. He wanted to write about the quaint and curious customs and habits of the people of the Transkei. He does it in a fairly benign way,[3] so it isn't the kind of regular *volkekunde* stuff, but he can't get out of that.

J: What's the more malignant?—

M: It's to use it to kind of ... as tied to the apartheid system. To actually work out who the people are who belong to which tribe, and which chief held the administration together. That's the kind of malignant stuff, which was the Native Administration's function of a lot of the early anthropology. Durban, as I said, was the more liberal stuff ... with Eileen Krige at the helm, and Caroline White later, and Jim Kiernan, and Eleanor Preston-Whyte, and a guy called John Argyle who came out of the British and social anthropology traditions—which doesn't mean they didn't still think

---

[3] More recently, however, Spiegel has explained that other anthropologists have confronted Lamla's take on the traditionality of factional violence in the context of the Marikana Commission of enquiry. Given the political and social implications of Marikana in South Africa, the 'benignness' of such an approach may be called into question.

in neat, ethnic categories. Because, I mean, Monica did write about the Pondo as if they were kind of a relatively, neatly [defined] 'people', and uh … Krige about the Zulu … So you've got these kinds of—it isn't a neat distinction—but [the more malignant kind was] designed to … administer. Radcliffe-Brown's ideas about the mixes that were occurring are there in Monica's work early on. Look at the title of her book, *Reaction to Conquest*: these people are not just there, they're part of a population that is being subjected to an outside influence.

So [those are the universities] up the coast, and then going inland you have the University of Venda, created again as a Bantustan university for the Venda people. Again, their anthropology department was populated primarily by teachers who came out of the *volkekunde* tradition—mostly out of Pretoria because … for a long time *volkekunde* was actually based in Pretoria. Although it started in Stellenbosch, it shifted its base/home to Pretoria. So then you've got Venda, you've got another university, the University of the North, which was ostensibly for the Pedi in Turfloop, and so, again, the same sort of thing: another 'bush college', another place where the staff came mostly out of the *volkekunde* departments and continued to teach that approach. Heading south, you have the University of Pretoria, which had become the home of *volkekunde*. Then you've got the University of Witwatersrand, very much in the Radcliffe-Brown tradition all along, like UCT. The University of Potchefstroom … um … just hold on as regards the University of Johannesburg—which was called the Rand Afrikaans University—just hold on for that one for a bit.

The University of Potchefstroom was known as the *Potchefstroomse Universiteit vir Hoer Christelike Onderwys*: 'Potchefstroom University for Higher Christian Education'. So very much in the Dutch Reform Church space, *volkekunde* dominated, but one person in there called Fanie van Rensburg was trying to break out all along. [He] came out of *volkekunde*, but realised it didn't work … and kept on trying to break away from it. He's retired in the last couple of years, but he's remained, sort of active … and, partly because he worked with coloured people in Potchefstroom, so he knew [*volkekunde*] wasn't going to work, somehow, the stuff didn't work for him. Free State, another home of *volkekunde*, and that was linked to its being Afrikaans; Potchefstroom is still white-Afrikaans … was there a University of Bophuthatswana? Yes there was, I'm not sure they ever had an anthropology department. I don't think they did. Um … I think that was it … Let's talk about UNISA.

First, UNISA was—I'm not sure why—quite a big department … lots of correspondence students, and [it] had archaeology as well, and … I think partly because they appointed Berthold Pauw … he came out of Philip Mayer's lot, and also out of the missionary fold—he himself was a missionary. He got into anthropology, worked with Philip Mayer, so he understood the Radcliffe-Brownian stuff. He wasn't an Afrikaner nationalist, but tried to kind of straddle the two [social anthropology and *volkekunde*]. So UNISA was always the kind of place where, for many years an attempt was made to bridge the two approaches … there was no association with either the *volkekundiges* or social anthropologists as members. There was just an annual conference at which senior academics from both met—excluding Monica who reportedly refused to participate—and it was always held at UNISA because that was regarded as a kind of neutral space. Nowhere else could work. And it was very strictly controlled; who could attend that conference. You had to be teaching at a university, teaching anthropology, or have a PhD in anthropology from a recognised university. Somebody once came—the story goes—to one of those conferences with a PhD in anthropology from Oxford [but not teaching anthropology]. And the leading Afrikaans guys wanted to know, "Have we ever heard of this as a legitimate place to get a PhD in anthropology"—something so ridiculous. Martin West, if you ever get to meet him, interview him, he'll give you that story in more detail. John Sharp might remember it as well.

"I was what they would have called an 'opstoker'
... a provocateur ..."

J: How would they manage to avoid arguments enough to have a conference?

M: I don't know. I never went to one of those conferences. I was too young, too junior. The first one of those I ever attended was as a Master's student and it wasn't there, it was the first one that they agreed to run away from the UNISA campus. It was held here, in 1979, because it was some big anniversary for the University of Cape Town. I'm not sure how many years it was anymore, 150, one hundred and something? I don't know what it was. They agreed to have [the conference] here. But, until then, students weren't allowed to attend. And then [the conference steering committee members] were told, "Look, you can't possibly have a conference on this campus where you exclude the students. People are registered—post-graduate students in the department should be entitled to attend. Otherwise you're going to have them protesting outside". That was partly because they knew me, and I probably would have.

So there I was at UCT, and I remember going to this thing. They agreed that we could show up—I remember sitting in a lecture theatre in the Leslie building when the fellow from Potchefstroom, the head of the department, a fellow called van der Wateren, was presenting his stuff. It was straight *volkekunde* stuff. And I didn't really know what it was, we hadn't actually engaged with it. This was before John [Sharp] had written [a history of it], and we didn't really know what we were hearing, but it just ... everything seemed wrong about it and I just couldn't quite ... but I asked him kind of pointed questions.

[At the time] I was busy just finishing, or had just submitted ... I think what was the first Marxist anthropology in this country as a Master's dissertation, in '79. It was on Lesotho and migrant labour, but it was using the neo-Marxist models to do the analysis. I was arguing strongly for seeing everybody as interconnected, the whole; one capitalist mode of production dominated the whole of South Africa, and that kind of stuff. And here were these guys; and I stood at the back—my dissertation had been submitted I think, but hadn't been approved yet—and I was asking questions. The person who was chairing didn't know my name. He asked my name, so I said, "Spiegel", and I became 'Dr. Spiegel', because it was incomprehensible to them that anybody who wasn't at least a 'Dr. Something' would be questioning the professor in that sort of way. I had experienced something like that a little while earlier when I went to Port Elizabeth to attend an attempt to at a conference of anthropology students. I was an Honours student and I went ... we'd had an invitation. They had their professor do the keynote opening address, at the end of which, the chair of their association, who was chairing the session ... the professor presented and came to an end; The chair said, "Thank you very much", and then ended the session. And I went to him afterwards and said, "What's going on?! Don't you ask questions here? Don't you have discussions and stuff?" And he said, "That was the professor". I said "Yes, but ... but discussion time?" to which he responded: "We don't ask the professor questions". [That was in] 1975. And the other conference at UCT was '79, so I knew what to expect once I got in there. And I suppose my lecturers here, because I was ... I had this big bushy hair—

J: I was going to ask if you had long hair, wore a beret or something, surely?

M: Oh yeah, I had big bushy hair and a big beard ... Henk Pauw ... he sort of tells the story about when I first arrived at the Port Elizabeth student conference in 1975. He was a very junior lecturer there at the time. I was an Honours student though we're the same age; but remember, I had spent that time at Wits so I was a little bit older than the rest of the students. He says that the fellow who was the professor at the time took one look at me and said,

56

"We gotta get this guy and turn him upside down and use him as a toilet brush".

J: Do you think he meant it endearingly?

M: No, no, meanly, though Henk Pauw tells it jokingly now. Um, but it wasn't meant to be nice. I was what they would have called an '*opstoker*' ... a provocateur ...

Anyway, to get back to these various universities: the University of Johannesburg, or what was [then] Rand Afrikaans University was like the other new universities. It was set up in the '60s, directly across the road from the University of Witwatersrand to begin with. Um, an old site where the breweries had been, literally across the road ... and it was called the Rand Afrikaans University because the Witwatersrand University, like Rhodes, was [considered] too liberal, too English, and [the apartheid state] had to have a place where ... they didn't want to make them go to Pretoria. There were lots of Afrikaans speakers in Jo'burg and around there so they had to have their own Afrikaans language university. And again the anthropology department that was created there was a *volkekunde* department.

But here is the tricky bit, the interesting bit: as the original professor retired, a guy ... the [man who wrote about the Pedi] uh ... H.O. Mönnig ... As he retired the new people who took over from him ... the fellow in charge was a very bright *volkekundige,* but he couldn't handle working from within that paradigm .... A man called Kotzé, Boet Kotzé, J.C Kotzé. I've never know his given first name, always knew him as Boet. He turned anthropology around, turned the department around. And he and Kees van der Waal—Kees also came out of Pretoria, straight down the line *volkekundiges*—they turned it around into social anthropology, along with another colleague, A.T. Fischer, who was called 'At'.

And they were ridiculed, scorned by their friends, their peers, their teachers, everybody—for doing that. And then they established a new relationship with us. They came and visited here, we visited—I spent a few weeks, a week I think, teaching in their department. John Sharp did [too], I think Martin West might have as well—to try and just open things up a bit. It was … they really were revolutionary. I mean, in a way that my revolutionary position was hardly difficult to adopt … I didn't have to fight very hard. They did. They really struggled, and, I mean, you need to probably talk to Kees. You gotta get that stuff from Kees directly, about his experience of coming out of *volkekunde* and the struggle with that. Boet Kotzé too found it difficult and eventually resigned and went to farm; something that At Fischer may also have done. They were also very devout, very devoted church people, Boet, Kees, and At. If you go to Kees' home for a meal, there's always grace with all around the table holding hands before the meal. And yet … ah, not 'yet' I suppose, they didn't break away from their religious stuff. They actually said that that was what was driving them toward social anthropology, and away from *volkekunde*.

That's interesting stuff. Monica Wilson was also a church person. Her father was a missionary. And she wrote two kinds of stuff. She wrote academic stuff, which didn't express her opinions in any direct way; and she wrote stuff that was more popular, with most of it being published in *South African Outlook,* a publication of the South African … I think the SA Council of Churches! Her son, Francis, who is an economist, was the editor of *SA Outlook* for a long time. So there's a long history of involvement with the church. Jim Kiernan, at Durban, had been a priest, a Roman Catholic priest. I don't think Hammond-Tooke had much connection with the church, I don't think so.

J: I find that so interesting. My own religious background … it fading away was part of my gaining a social science consciousness of sorts. I have a hard time understanding how some theorists manage to …

M: Yeah, I also do—for me it's exactly the same. But they do. They really do. Victor Turner was a practicing Catholic, Evans-Pritchard was … Monica was very much a practicing Anglican … Michael Whisson at Rhodes continues to be a lay preacher in the cathedral at Grahamstown.

Chapter 5

Anthropology under Apartheid

"One of the major activist roles was to teach students ..."

J: What were the circumstances of David Webster's assassination?

M: He was ... it was a guy called Ferdi Barnard [a member, it later turned out, of the apartheid era Civil Cooperation Bureau]. And it was probably because he was regarded ... he was very involved with The Detainees' Parents' Support Committee (DPSC) and with the End Conscription Campaign, both of which were part of the ANC in exile, in a way, and part of the UDM movement. And I think he also discovered a whole lot of stuff doing research in northern Natal ... around arms, arms movements between South Africa to the RENAMO people in Mozambique, the anti-FRELIMO movement, I think. About that I have no ... I don't think there's any evidence about that, but that maybe he *knew*, maybe he *did* write, I don't know. Maybe he didn't know, but they just assumed he did, but he was regarded as somebody who shouldn't be around and was assassinated on May Day ... in 1989, outside his house .... May Day wasn't a formally celebrated day here before apartheid fell because it was regarded as a communist inspired holiday, and we in SA were of course against the communists. McCarthy would have done well in this country.

J: Did much argument for activism come up in the '80s? Over whether anthropologists should be activists in the struggle?

M: Of course. Yeah it did. I mean, we saw ourselves as activists—in 1990, the second of February, when de Klerk made his speech to say that he was going to release Nelson Mandela, unban the ANC and the PAC and everything else, and slowly release all the political prisoners and move towards something else, a new arrangement ... Martin West—in what's now [the present Head of Department's] office—and John Sharp, Emile Boonzaier, and I sat there listening to the radio, to hear the speech. At the end of it we looked at each other and said, "What are we gonna do now?"

Because our whole *raison d'être* had gone. Everything we were doing ... I mean from 1973 or so, when I first started doing stuff, was driven by a concern to show-up what the apartheid state was doing. To try and provide the evidence, expose their stuff. And we said, "Now what?" And we still haven't quite found out. It was easy—it was much easier to be able to identify the enemy [before then]. It was easy. Van der Wateren was the fellow from Potchefstroom that I went for at the [1979] conference. *He* represented it. The state represented it. They were there, you could see them, they were people, it wasn't neoliberal principles as we have now to target. It wasn't 'The Washington Consensus'. It wasn't things like that. It was a small, narrow-minded government, and a bunch of narrow-minded anthropologists and others who supported them. It was much easier to know who your enemy was. Now it's this diffuse idea. ... Um ... So, yeah, that was what drove us ... which didn't mean we were necessarily there on the streets.

In a way my own experience of protest politics was such that I didn't want to be on the streets. It didn't, I found, really make a whole lot of difference—I did do a bit of it when I first came here to UCT. I got sort of close to the NUSAS people who were banned, including our [present-day] dean [Paula Ensor], who was a NUSAS leader who was banned in 1973. And she went into exile. She was in exile for a long time. And she was thrown out of the ANC for being too left wing. Yeah. And, to my mind, she hasn't actually shifted ideologically on most things, it's just a matter of trying to make it work more, it's more pragmatic. But she's—I have enormous respect for her. Um ... but, so our role—one of the major activist roles was to teach students.

We [had] these almost all white students. ['Non-white'] students weren't allowed into the university [at the time], except for very few. It began to loosen up sometime in the early '80s ... but still, even then, it was relatively few. You had a few coloured students who could get in because there were certain courses which weren't offered by UWC. They were called permit courses, you could get a permit—Crain Soudien, [UCT's present] Deputy Vice-Chancellor, whom I tutored, came to UCT, a coloured guy, from Johannesburg originally. He managed to get into UCT because he did Comparative African Government and Law (CAGL), which was a course that wasn't offered at UWC, so he could say, "I'm doing that, that's my main goal, to do that stuff!" And so he got into UCT and then could do other courses because they were part of his degree. There [was] a permit to be allowed to register, and the permit was issued if they were accepted into the permit courses ... Most—I mean if someone wanted to do science—couldn't get in here ... A couple of people managed to get in that way, but most people found that it was just very restrictive. I mean, the kids coming into our first year class were kids who ... were white, almost all ... white South Africans who were relatively affluent, and who knew nothing at all about what was going on in their country! At all. I mean, the relocation stuff that was happening and we were documenting in the 1980s. They didn't have the first inkling of the migrant labour stuff either.

J: You still get students today who are really surprised to read those works from [the early '80s], like that stuff about the Bantustans, 'jigsaws that do not fit' ...

M: That's right! Yeah, Colin Murray, who wrote that, wasn't allowed in the country. He used to sneak in ... he'd go to Lesotho and come across the border there ...

J: Where was that published then?

M: That stuff of his was published or at least available here, you could—*he* wasn't allowed in the country, but his stuff wasn't banned.

J: So the university still, at that time—was there pressures about publishing certain things …

M: Um, you must see if you can find a copy of that book, *Oxford History of South Africa.* [Pulls down a book off the shelf] Not this one, cause I went to Lesotho and bought this one. But at the time, the second volume of it included an article by … Leo Kuper … That's right, 'African Nationalism in South Africa' [1910-1964]. A whole lot of these books were published—that book was published and distributed in this country with blank pages for that chapter. Not a large number. A collector's item at this point if you can get your hands on one.

Leo Kuper himself wasn't banned, but some of the stuff he was quoting in there … they got legal advice and they were told they would end up with the whole book being disallowed because what he was [referencing] had been banned. Anybody who was … listed as having been a member of the Communist Party [which] was banned in 1960—anything that they wrote wasn't allowed to be distributed here. And a whole lot more … a hell of a lot more. The library used to get it, and to keep it in a special locked-up cabinet, and you could, with some effort, get permission as an academic to read some of that stuff.

So yes, it was difficult. None of our stuff was ever banned. Um … the closest I got to that was a scurrilous journal … which I was associated with in the sense that it was published under the name of the UCT Radical Society in my first year when the Radical Society (Radsoc) … well … I was the president. And how did I become president? Because we sat around a room and we tried to resuscitate the organisation—because at that stage, societies, and this might still be the case, got money from the student administration. And there was money waiting there but you had to have a committee. So we said, "Let's get this organisation back on track so we can get this money to do some stuff". There were two organisations like that; the other was called 'The Modern World Society'. We sat in a room in the basement of the Beattie [building] at lunchtime and we said, "We need presidents and a chair", or whatever it was, "vice-chair, and a secretary, and a treasurer", for each one, somebody then said [while pointing] "president-radical society, president ..." and I just happened to be sitting there and was pointed to as president ...

J: And you were the Radical Society president.

M: So I became, either president or chairman, I don't know. And then ... this must have been in '72, a guy called Philippe le Roux who had been involved in *Sax-Appeal*, editing *Sax-Appeal* [UCT's annual RAG magazine]. *Sax-Appeal* raises funds for SHAWCO, exclusively. And SHAWCO was coming to be regarded by some as a completely patronising organisation ... For SHAWCO, you've gotta find Johann Graaff, who's the sort of head of SHAWCO now. He's in the Department of Sociology as well; he'll give you that history. But SHAWCO, a number of us said, 'this is patronising!' You know, it isn't asking questions about what these kinds of organisations do, it's simply ameliorating conditions. It's anti-revolutionary because it's enabling people to survive against the odds, rather than to fight the odds.

So, there was a whole critique of SHAWCO; and Philippe le Roux, very naughtily, agreed to edit *Sax-Appeal*—he wanted to be in the journalism world—*but* he then took the editorial chunk of *Sax-Appeal* and wrote a scathing piece about SHAWCO in it. [The university authorities] got hold of it at the very last moment. It wasn't distributed, but they had to then reprint it. It cost a lot of money and he got into a lot of trouble. He was allowed to remain on campus, but he was banned from publishing anything on campus—that was part of his punishment for having abused his position as *Sax Appeal* editor. I mean it did cost the university quite a lot of money.

J: I could see it being sort of a badge of honour though, to [write something that's been] banned.

M: Well, for some of us it was. … There were people who sort of prided themselves on having had their passports removed and stuff like that. That kind of silly politics was also going on. "You're not bad enough, or not good enough to have been regarded as bad enough". I can myself sort of walk around 'proudly' and say, "I was refused permission to do research in the Transkei, so I went to Lesotho instead". Yeah, really in 1976 [radical students would compete and say things like], "but I always had a passport" [it was never removed by the state]. You know (Laughs). "I could always leave, I was never denied permission, and I was never banned and put under house arrest", or any of that kind of stuff …

But Philippe, we agreed to let him put together this broadsheet [as a Radsoc journal], though of course his name wouldn't be on it. But then he got involved with a national publication, with NUSAS, and didn't need to do something on campus, because he was doing something that was going to reach all the campuses. The person who was going to front for him was terribly disappointed that he had lost his opportunity for putting something out with his name on it. So he produced some really scurrilous garbage called 'Plop'. And it was, it was … distasteful, quite a lot of it, just … and so I got into trouble. It was banned; 'Plop' was banned by the state. There were 300 copies published, printed, I think, something like that. It was stupid. But they got hold of it and it was banned, and I got hauled before the vice-chancellor, rapped over the knuckles. I did say, "But I didn't do anything, I didn't distribute it, I didn't write it, I … he was the editor, this fellow, he was the editor". He was from Zimbabwe, or Rhodesia as it was then. He fled the country, because he didn't want to be thrown out of UCT or get into trouble; and he never came back. It was his last appearance on campus, a guy called Dan Meyer. That was as close as I got to anything that I was associated with being banned, as far as I know.

J: Do you know a lot of people who have come back from exile since then?

M: Quite a lot … Paula Ensor is the first that comes to mind …

J: Have more come back than not come back, or have more stayed away?

M: I don't know. I mean, you need to kind of separate out those who went into exile and those who, like Paula, who really couldn't do anything here. And others who went into exile because they were running away from … the draft or—

J: Imprisonment?

M: Not only imprisonment, but just because they didn't want to be in this context. I mean, I've got lots of friends who went away, um but it wasn't really … My brother is one, who left the country because he didn't want to have to go do more army [service], but it wasn't really a strong political position that he took. Um, and he lives in Canada … I don't regard him as somebody who went into exile the way that Paula Ensor went into exile, or Neville Curtis, also a NUSAS leader, or those people who were part of this, sort of … and Barry Gilder, who came back … there are a whole lot of those kind of people, and many of those people have come back. Those are the real exiles, the others I'm not sure. I would never call my brother 'a refugee', or [say he] 'went into exile'. He just was looking for a more comfortable place to live. And a hell of a lot of South African Jews did that, and that's partly why I make that distinction. They were running. They were frightened. And they went off to North America, some to Australia … and I don't regard them as exiles. I've got cousins in Australia, and cousins in the States. My brother is in Canada, my sister in London, and friends all over the world … mostly in Britain. My closest school friend is in Britain. That's the medical doctor I mentioned who led me to think I should study medicine in 1967/8.

M: I was in Soweto in 1976 on the 15th of June. And I wasn't there on the 16th of June [at the beginning of 'the Soweto Uprising'], because I had to do some stuff in town. I did go back either the 17th or the 18th ... um, to a hostel, and was sent away by the hostel manager who told me I wasn't allowed to be there. I said, "I've got a permit"—you had to have a permit, as a white person, to be in Soweto. And he said, "That has now been suspended" ... and I went off to town and got another one. I came back with the next one. But when they issued me with it they said, "all right", they'd give me another one, but I was going in strictly under my own ... what did they call it? ... "At your own risk".

J: Did you feel very at risk during your fieldwork?

M: No, never. The people I had been working with said to me when I went back after the 16th June, that if I'd have been there that day they would have hidden me away and probably smuggled me out in a car boot, or something like that. Whether that's what would have happened if I'd been there, who knows, but that's what they said. No, I never felt particularly at risk there. I've never felt massively at risk in any of the places I've been to. I feel more at risk sometimes on my own street. Because uh, there's more to take from where I am there. Of course, I'm kind of conscious of risk all the time. I've been in episodes, which are worthy of record, but they've got nothing to do with anthropology.

J: That doesn't matter!

M: Doesn't it? Okay. I'm not sure in what order, anymore. Um ... the only time I felt at risk in the field was in the Transkei. When I'd got permission to be there—again, I had to have a permit [a temporary residence visa after late 1976]—I'd been to the magistrate, got permission from him, he was the local sort of district administrator as well ... um ... and then suddenly one day the cops arrived, and took me away … early in the morning. [They] took me off with my assistant, who was a local woman, to the remote Ongeluksnek border post on the border between Lesotho and the Transkei, up in the mountains. It wasn't in the same district where I was, and it was relatively cold; and I thought, "Well, what are they gonna do with me here?" So I felt a little uneasy there, but I felt most uneasy when a vehicle arrived driven by … the South African security policeman in the nearby Matatiele town—which I knew I recognised. The kind of absurd part about it was that— because when I'd been picked up, I'd managed to get a note to a neighbour saying, "Please take this to the priest in town", who's an Englishman, who then phoned my wife. Um … here's a funny bit of it: [the priest's wife] said to her, on a cracking phone line, [that] her husband had been arrested. And she heard *"dead"*. She didn't hear that well. And she said, "What'd you say!?" She said she kind of got a bit of a shock to begin with, and she asked her to repeat herself and then she heard "arrested". And she said, "Oh, that's okay". She was so relieved that I was only arrested.

J: Did they tell you why they were taking you away, or where they were taking you?

M: …The Transkei at that point was independent, the first 'independent' Bantustan. And it was treasonable there to question the legitimacy of the independent Transkei, or its independence— something which I knew and so would never have said anything like that. Um … and they accused me of that, they accused me of mobilising people to question things, and [they said] I'd been at a meeting and I'd been at a gathering, which I hadn't. I'd never done any of it. But I was pretty sure I knew what was going on because, by that point, I'd realised that there was quite a big rift in the village. The headman, on whose property I lived, was at loggerheads with the woman who lived directly across the road and who had connections to some of the chiefs in the area, and also with the police. And she believed that her husband should have been the headman, not the man who was hosting me. She objected to my being on his property and not hers, because she reckoned he was going to use me and my car—which he didn't because he was a very decent man—but she would have! So I was very pleased I'd made the choice I had …

J: You ended up on the right side of the road.

M: But she … just basically called her friends in from the police to give me a bit of a shakeup, to frighten [my host] mostly. So it was very little to do with me. Um, and I realised that fairly soon that that was probably what was going on; and then, as I was being taken away by the police who were responsible for it, I heard them say to this woman [from across the road], "Well, now we've got him, what do you want us to do with him?"

So … I knew it was all bogus stuff. But, when the South African security police guy arrived where I was being held I thought, "Now there really is trouble". Because it happened around the same time as some other guys—that I knew quite well—in Mthatha, at the university, had been busted and deported from the Transkei for all sorts of stuff. And I thought, since I was associated with them, maybe it was linked with that—that was when the South African security police guy arrived. But then it turned out that, among the things the priest in town had done—remember, his wife had talked to my wife—he had also talked to a lawyer in town. [The lawyer] then went to the security police and said, "What is this? This is one of our citizens in a foreign country! You ought to talk to the Department of Foreign Affairs". So, there I was then, ostensibly being *looked after* by South African security police. My welfare was being checked on … that they weren't doing anything too dastardly to me … which was kind of completely um … for me … such a reverse of everything. Because, for me the South African security police were much more the enemy than the Transkei was.

Afterwards, when it was all over—it was only for fifteen or sixteen hours, then we were released—I went into town to talk to the priest and said, "Look I've been released and nothing's happening, so don't worry about it. Thank you for whatever you've done" … I went to talk to various people … including the security police guy … to say, "Well, what did you know?" I was trying to find out what he knew about what happened. And he told me very little, but then [he] tried to interrogate me. Not nastily, but sort of … "Well, why *were* you there?!" and I said, "Well, I don't know!"

So … then I went, a couple days later, to Mthatha [then called 'Umtata']—which was the capital of the Transkei—to see the South African ambassador. I'd been told I should go and thank him for his efforts too. So I arrived unannounced, was ushered in within minutes to his office. Clearly he didn't have much to do. Um … Melissa Steyn's father—Marais Steyn it was—Melissa Steyn [is] in Sociology [and] runs the Diversity Studies Program[4]— … I was ushered in to [see] him. His first secretary was also there, so clearly they *really* didn't have much to do. I said, "Listen, this is who I am; this is why I've come. I just wanted to say thank you and to find out what *you* know about what this was about". They said, "Well, we've talked to the [Transkei] police again this morning to find out what this was all about, and they said that the person concerned"—they didn't say "you"—"was actually arrested and charged and was out on bail". And I said, "Well, not me then, they're talking about somebody else because I've not paid a penny, and I've not seen a charge of any kind, so … I'm not sure what we're talking about here". And they also said … "There was some altercation between him and a woman in the village and … he pissed on the woman's pig and now the pig has got an eye infection". Literally, those were ambassador Steyn's words.

And I looked at him and I said, "Look, for a start, this altercation with the woman bit, if that implies I've been unfaithful to my wife, I absolutely deny it, ever, haven't been". I said, "But, you know, those little pigs that run around in the Transkei villages? They don't stand still long enough for you to piss on them, let alone get it into the eye!" And we all just laughed. So … when I came back, in my leave report, I included that story, so that somewhere in the university archives you might find my leave report from the 1980s, '84 probably. It was a sabbatical leave …

---

[4] At the time of these interviews, Melissa Steyn held a position at UCT, but now is involved in the Diversity Studies Program at Wits.

J: Where you report that you were accused of pissing on a pig?

M: Yeah. Just because I thought I had to make, sort of to give the [whole story]—and the vice chancellor at the time used to read those leave reports. So it kind of went all the way to the top ... this junior guy in the anthropology department pissed on a pig ... and later some anthropology students produced a little newsletter with an image of the whole imagined scene ...

> *"He happened to be black, they happened to be white.*
> *And I intervened"*

M: But then ... two incidents which I will just tell you about South Africa, but not about anthropology here: one of them was flying up to Jo'burg many years ago, before the fall of apartheid ... but there were already black traffic officers in Jo'burg ... Which is important because of the way the story goes.

My father picked me up at the airport, drove me to where his business was based, on ... the southeastern edge of the city centre. I [was going to] drop him off at work and go off with his car. As we got close to the place, at the last intersection, the traffic lights turned red and we stopped. And, as we stopped, a young man came running up the road and ran straight into the side of the car. He wasn't looking where he was going. [He was] looking behind him, was running really fast, and flipped right over the car. He hit the side [of the car] and then flipped right to the other side, and hurt himself a bit ... So I jumped out of the car to see what was going on; and some other young men came running up after him and grabbed hold of him. He happened to be black, they happened to be white. And I intervened. I said, "What the hell are you doing? This guy's just had a motorcar accident, a traffic accident, and now you're trying to drag him away. What's going on?! I've gotta call the traffic police". [They then said] "He was trying to steal our car ... down over there, on the side of the road and ... we were upstairs in

70

our workshop, two floors up, and we saw him trying to break into the car and so we shot at him and then came chasing after him". They didn't actually tell me about the shooting yet at that point.

So I said, "Well we've gotta call the traffic police, there's been an accident". I said to my father, "You just go inside, call the traffic police, and I'm gonna go with these people and see where they're gonna take this guy, because they have no right to do this" ... They took him up into their workshop, which was a sort of small, metalwork place ... and ... they were gonna beat the hell out of him; but now I was there. Whether or not he did try to break into their car, I have no idea. Their boss then arrived, an older man, Italian. And he got really angry that I was intervening. By this stage, I had managed to convince the younger guys to let me hold the fugitive in a separate room, away from them, where neither of us could get out, and they would call the police and the police would deal with it. So I, being a little bit older than they, managed to swing this, but then the boss arrived and he was angry. He was probably my age, or maybe a bit older—

J: And what kind of building was this?

M: It was a small industrial building. My father's business had originally been on the ground floor of the same building ... A warehouse, sort of large, where each floor was a warehouse of its own ... My father had a wholesale hardware business and he used the main warehouse part as a warehouse, literally shelves and shelves full of tools. And he'd moved around the corner, bought another building of his own ... and moved in there. It was literally two minutes' walk away. So I was up there with them right when my father came up, and he must have been ... probably not quite eighty [years old] ... at that point. He saw me, but then saw the boss with the gun—the boss had pulled out a gun—he was really angry. It turned out that they'd actually shot across a busy road at somebody at their car, they claimed it was [this man].

The boss got really cross and waved his gun around ... the guy that they'd sort of held was hiding behind me [now], so I was the human shield—between [him and] this madman with a gun ...

71

Having pulled it out of his boot holster—and having it in his hand—[the boss seemed to feel] he had to do something with it. He couldn't not—and eventually he discharged it into the floor. And the bullet ricocheted all over the place. I was pretty frightened. But nothing actually hit anybody ... but then ...

J: This guy was willing to pull out a gun and make a big scene just because someone tried to break into his car?

M: Maybe! To this day I have no idea whether anybody ever did! Whether he might have just been walking up, he might have stopped and looked in the car, who knows what actually happened! It might have been somebody else—who knows! I mean I never got to the bottom of what really happened. All I know is that they had shot across the road, they had said so, and then they wanted to beat the hell out of [this man]. They said that their cars had been broken into, or stolen or something, recently, so they were kind of alert to the possibility.

Then the traffic police; and the police arrived. The police arrived in the form of two young, very wiry, white men. Because, at that point black police were relatively few and far between, and didn't deal with the white part of the city. Um, but the traffic officers, traffic police, were somewhat older, burlier, and both black ... I think the traffic officers arrived first, I told them what had happened I said, "This guy [the boss] has broken the law. He's discharged his firearm in a built-up area for no good reason. I don't [know] about the others. They say they shot—or there is some story of shooting. I didn't see it, so I can only tell you what I've heard. But this I know: he discharged his firearm into the floor. It ricocheted all over the place, completely unnecessary in this built-up area. It's illegal".

Then the [other] police arrived, and there was a bit of tension between the black traffic officers and the police—the wiry white guys—they were younger; and eventually they said, "Well we're gonna take everybody—all of them in—to sort this out" ... And I said, "But you can't put those same people together—in the back of the van—because they'll beat the shit out of him!" And so they put

72

the white guys into the back of the van and the black guy into the back of the traffic officers' car. So he got a soft ride. To where, I don't know. It was the last I ever heard of them. I gave them all my details in case they wanted to pull me in as a witness or something, but nothing ever happened. So that's my one frightening incident to do with guns.

"More frightening [were] the people in authority, the administrators, cause they didn't want me there, cause they were terrified"

J: I'm sure that story has something to do with anthropology ...

M: But never doing fieldwork. I went back into Soweto [immediately following the 1976 Uprising, for example]. More frightening was the people in authority, the administrators, cause they didn't want me there, cause they were terrified. Um, and they were nasty to me. But ... the people in Soweto that I met were not frightening. I used to be asked, "Do you carry a firearm with you when you go off to the Transkei?" And I'd say, "What for?" And they'd say, "Well, to protect yourself". And I said, "But, I don't like them. I've never owned one. I had to carry one in the military, but I wouldn't ... it'd probably be taken off me and used against me, so why would I carry such a thing around?" That's been my attitude and I've never ever felt a desperate need to have one, or to have one to protect myself.

... But I mean—in the position I am in now, and previously as a Head of a Department—you do have to be ... cautious with where your students go. And to remind them to be alert and cautious and not to ... let themselves get into situations that could be dangerous. The way to deal with it is, if it's getting—looks—problematic, rather leave! As exciting as it might be to watch the action, rather go away. Your life is more important than your thesis. When Fiona [Ross] did her first fieldwork in the shack settlement, which becomes the book *Raw Life, New Hope* later, the arrangement was that she would phone me before she went ... and I'd need to know how long she was going to be there. Then she'd phone me when she got home. But, very often she didn't, and I'd be more panicky than she. It's actually much worse when you're not there. Because you don't know what could be happening. When you're in the place, you're kind of relatively in control of things. Obviously not complete control.

But, yeah, we had those kinds of arrangements in place. And now that Jonathan (Jessica's classmate) heads off to Barcelona (a nearby township), I kind of have to say, "Jonathan …just …"—cause he's a bit of a hot-heated fellow anyway—"just keep cool. Don't do anything silly there" … But then, I would say the same if he were working in the city council offices, cause he could antagonise people. So … one has to be kind of diplomatic, or as close to that as possible, which I'm not always very good at.

J: So do you think doing fieldwork in a township in Cape Town, for example, has changed at all since you were doing research in Soweto?

M: I think so, I think there's much more … well, crime has been there in large scale, it just wasn't recorded. People died every single day—Groote Schuur [Hospital], or uh … it's no longer there anymore, Conradie Hospital. People have come from Europe, and particularly Germany, to those hospitals—for trauma surgery experience—for thirty years or more!

Again an example from my father's business … he didn't start it but he moved into a tiny little business, which he then built up and took over. There was one black man who was working there almost as long as my father. He was there long before my father was married, long before I came along … And, he lived in Soweto. And one Monday he didn't come back to work. A very decent fellow, in every best sense. He would go home with his wages and hand over his wages to his wife, and go and see a friend. He went off to see a friend, and he got knocked off for his wages. And that must have been, oh I don't know, late '50s, early '60s … ugh. And that's, I mean, that was not an unusual kind of incident—just no one ever reported it, certainly not the press. And the police records were, 'ah well, just another black guy, so what, who cares'? So, it was there, that kind of violence and crime has been there a long time.

"Who knows?"

J: I was intrigued by a point that Jean and John Comaroff made when they visited ... that [during apartheid], at least you sort of knew who your enemy was and it was mostly the state ... whereas today there's this feeling of uncertainty ... you don't know who to blame. Right after that seminar I attended a funeral in the township where I had done much of my fieldwork, where there was all this ... uncertainty about this guy and why he was killed. He had been called out of his house early in the morning, I think at five am or so—someone called him by name to come outside and he came outside and [someone] shot him in the head and then ran off. And people were saying, "He had just gotten involved in politics, he had just gotten a higher position in COPE [Congress of the People]", so some thought it was politically motivated. But then there were also these guys—tsotsis—who were known for hanging out around the street corner near his block. So then, it could have just been that. Because this guy [who was shot] had a reputation for kind of chasing them off if they were bothering some of the women in the community, so everyone was so upset when he was killed because he was kind of this respected community figure, but this ... just being left with ... [sigh] not knowing who or why. It was an interesting point to say that that was particularly different from how things were during apartheid, because the state was the clear enemy, but I'm not sure that—

M: Well, for some of us it was. For me it was ... and I suppose for the liberal white establishment it was. But for people in the township it wasn't only that. They had to be fearful of *tsotsis*, because *tsotsis* go back a long time. Um, and the state simply encouraged that sometimes. And certainly Cape Town did ... encouraged local chiefs or self appointed headmen to take control of areas and then allocate bits of land for people to put up their shacks. And then they became like local leaders, warlords, and they mobilised people to fight against others. And the police encouraged it.

But you didn't know—you don't always know who your enemy is. And one of the difficulties of growing up, being a youngster in the period of apartheid, was that, as a student—I might have said this to you before—there were often moments when ...with a group of people ... you didn't know whether to say very much. We all did, we all had the same fears. If you said too much then you were a provocateur. If you said too little then you were just snooping. Um, and you didn't know who in the bunch was the informer. Or whether there was one at all ... and that's really horrible, to be with your friends and worry that one of them might be a police spy.

J: That just seems so unfamiliar to me. And I suppose is one of those things that would really characterise being under a repressive state, to be in that situation.

M: Yes. Yeah. And also not knowing if somebody would point a finger at you and say, "You're it". Because how do you prove you aren't if you're accused of it. There were two people in ... there was one who was banned with the NUSAS-eight called Chris Wood, on the grounds that he was always around them, and nobody ever knew what he was up to ... said the state, so he must be problematic. He was always around with these people, wasn't part of the executive, but wherever there was something going on, he was there.

J: Who were 'these people?' Meaning NUSAS?

M: The NUSAS leaders. Chris Wood. And for exactly the same reason, some people in the movement suspected Chris Wood of being a police informer. He was banned, and he continued to live in

76

a house with Neville Curtis, who was then the president of NUSAS. Of course, they technically weren't allowed to see each other. Now one could say, "Well, they were just thumbing their noses at the state"; or the state could have been saying, "Well, let's leave Chris Wood there so he can keep on watching"—to this day, who knows? I don't know what happened to Chris Wood. Neville Curtis went to Australia and has died since .... Um ... Who knows? And there were others like that, sort of, who were there, but not quite formally involved. And people would say, "Well ... we don't know why this guy's involved ..." so it's awful stuff. But anyway, that's not anthropology in the sense of my research.

It certainly didn't ... I suppose it had some influence on the way I ...I became ... sort of, my attitude in anthropology, but it wasn't what ... took me into anthropology. That was really ... as I've told you before, being excited. Being able to find ... the economics that I wanted to do, not the economics that I was being taught by UCT economists in the course they offered. And then having the opportunity to keep going to Lesotho, which I kind of, at one point, thought was going to be kind of my ... spiritual home, or something like that. And I felt very much more at home there than in South Africa.

J: I think a lot of anthropologists ... have a similar ... feeling or calling to where they did their first research.

M: Mmmm, mmm .... Yeah, I mean, that's why, I suppose, Fiona [Ross] ended up back in the same population that she wrote the recent book about, because ... that was her first sense of really being embedded in ... and my relationship with Lesotho goes back before anthropology with that voluntary service stuff. So ... and opportunities came along, also. And my Honours, I told you, was ... Martin West, called me one day and said, "You go to Lesotho all the time. Here's an opportunity. Go and do it". And that sort of set me on the way. Had that not happened, who knows?

Chapter 6

Tradition in Transition

"So, it's a whole set of circumstances which have changed it"

J: How did things start to change at UCT? Especially between '76 and the mid-'80s? You've said you were the first one to write a really neo-Marxist—

M: —'79, I introduced the neo-Marxist analysis into a dissertation ...um ... and I think the first in an anthropology dissertation in the country ... because, there were really very few post-graduate students in the country, certainly in anthropology.

J: They all went elsewhere?

M: Yeah, well, there weren't many going anywhere. In anthropology, I mean—as I said I was the only Honours student in my year. The year after me, there were three or four, I think, the year before me there was just one, and the year before that there were three. Wits had three the year before I was based there during my Rhodes job, maybe one or two the year that I was there, so it was very small and then most people didn't go on to do Master's degrees. So it was, I mean, when I did mine I think there were two of us that were registered: Sally Frankental and me. And Emile Boonzaier then, and Sally had been at it for some time.

J: So is this maybe the biggest—at this point in time, that this department has ever been?

M: In terms of students? Post-graduate students? *Way* the biggest! I mean we've got ... last year's Honours class was the biggest ever: seventeen. Twelve had been the biggest before that, now I think we've got thirteen or fourteen.[5] Um, Master's, we didn't have a coursework Master's until 1997, I think. Till then it was dissertation only. And, it was few … it was Sally and me, and then Emile … And PhDs, none. There was one every few years. And then along comes … Mamphela Ramphele, and Pamela Reynolds— who started at Cambridge and then switched to Cape Town—but again it was relatively few. Twenty-three we've got now, on the books, PhDs, which is kind of … unthinkable! When I was head of the department [1999-2008] it was thirteen at one point, and I, we, couldn't believe it, and now it's nearly twice that.

J: Do you think there's been a big change in what draws people to anthropology?

M: I think there's a bigger—another—change first that's important, and that is that there are more people wanting post-graduate degrees. There's been a devaluation of degrees. When I was at high school, most people got a 'matric', so the weak ones got a JC, a 'junior certificate' …. Most people would try to get a matric and that was it. Some went to university and got a degree. And then it became anybody who was anything got a matric, and then some went to university … so the JC became the matric, and then the first degree became like matric, and the Honours then became … and so it keeps on. There's an inflation in that. And you see it in post-docs … it wasn't a concept [previously]. And now you've got a doctorate *and* then you do a post-doc. It just wasn't there. And there are also more people in the world now, making the demand ever greater.

So there are all sorts of outside imperatives which are causing this growth … but why people are coming to anthropology? I think it's partly that. I'm not sure it's *because* it's anthropology. It's that more people are looking for post-graduate qualifications. And we're certainly getting a bigger number than some of our peer UCT departments. I mean we have far more PhDs registered than History, and Religious Studies … we have, right now in 2011, about

---

[5] There were twenty-seven Honours students registered with UCT Anthropology at the beginning of 2014.

the same number as Sociology and they have twice the number of staff as we've got. Yet, those things kind of come and go. Sociology at this university has been weak for a very long time. And it's actually probably at its strongest since the early '70s, and in the early '70s PhDs were not worried about except for the one or two people who went on to teach, and then only once you were teaching. So, it's a whole set of circumstances which have changed it.

J: Yeah, the university system altogether, not just anthropology. And you mentioned Ramphele—

M: She has a PhD from this department. Um, Mamphela has a medical degree, a first degree ... did a thesis supervised by Martin West in this department. She has a ... first degree as a medical doctor. She was banished by the apartheid regime for quite a while and wasn't allowed to practise for a bit, I think, and so she did a commerce administration-type thing with UNISA. When that came to an end she [came] to UCT because of Francis Wilson who brought her in as a researcher and a sort of co-leader of the work being done on the 1980s Carnegie poverty commission. There had been an [earlier] poverty commission funded by the Carnegie Foundation, a big poverty commission uh, in the 1920s, which was really about poor whites. It wasn't to do with black people, coloured people, sort of 'the scourge of poverty' for people who shouldn't be like that: white people. Black people, eh, "they're primitives, they've stayed like that".

J: Like Zine Magubane's piece, where white people are acting like 'the uncivilised natives', 'better fix them'.

M: That's right. Francis Wilson managed to get a very large amount of money, for the time, out of the Carnegie Foundation to do another one, which was for the whole country. There was a big conference in 1984. It wasn't the same kind of commission with a few people doing the research and writing a report. It was ... I think, hundreds, some hundreds of papers, all sorts of people doing something on poverty in South Africa. This department [UCT Anthropology] I think produced more papers as a unit than any other unit anywhere in the world. ... Yeah, of various kinds, we had a whole lot of students doing work on it. They were all Honours students, maybe some Master's students too by then. [Ramphele] was brought in to help coordinate that all for the whole conference and do research on it, and eventually Francis Wilson and she put together the summary volume from all of that stuff, they worked through this whole massive pile of papers and other stuff and produced a book.

At the end of that she decided she wanted a PhD, and she talked around and found Martin West who was willing to supervise her through it. She then chose a topic, which was with hostel dwellers in the townships here. Partly health related, it was sort of medical anthropology, but also about conditions in the hostels generally. So it was again poverty-related. The hostels had been created as places for black men to come and live while they worked here and then [would] go back to where 'they belonged' at home, in the Bantustans. By then, by the early '80s, there'd been a kind of ... a resistance to forcing spouses and children to stay in the Bantustans, so the townships had grown. There were more and more shack settlements rising up and being demolished and coming up again. People were put on trains and buses back to the Eastern Cape and then simply turning around when they got there and coming back. Many of the men in the hostels managed to bring their wives and children in, and what you had were these really horrible little spaces, made for two men to live in, very small little rooms, two beds, window, little table, maybe, between the two beds, and then a wire cage at the end for each to have a locker for a bit of clothing. When Mamphela was doing the research in the late '80s, you found fourteen people living in a room like that ... A book called *A Bed Called Home*. Um, it's really freaky stuff. And we all went and helped and did some of the interviewing for her.

She put that together into a PhD ... Soon after that she moved on to become a ... deputy vice chancellor, and then became the vice chancellor ... and then left that to go become a Vice-President [of External Affairs] ... at the World Bank. Ramphele ... but she

82

wasn't the first black woman in [this] department. Harriet Ngubane was here before that; she was an anthropologist—She ... I think was a schoolteacher to begin with, from KwaZulu-Natal, taken up through the system at the University of Natal, and then—I think she has a Cambridge PhD—and then couldn't find a job here because she was a black woman.

J: But they didn't have sit-ins for her?

M: No ... because it was much later now—

J: —because Mafeje was accepted, but then they turned him down afterwards?

M: Yeah, it was very clear. I mean, they—the state and the universities—had learnt their lesson once, they weren't going to go there again. I remember seeing Harriet Ngubane in Lesotho ... the UCT vice-chancellor then decided to try and bring her on board as a special advisor in the UCT administration. This would have been, I don't know, '85, '86 ... but it didn't work for long; the agreement was that she would be a supernumerary person in this department, and, if it didn't work out in the UCT administration, she would simply come up here and become part of us. As it turned out, it didn't really work there, and she suddenly became part of our department. It didn't hurt in the sense that we had her alongside us; but it was difficult because she ... she didn't like the kind of anthropology we were doing because she was an old uh ... Inkatha Freedom person. She wanted to—the Zulu *ethnos* was more important to her than the national, [than] South Africa as a single nation. And so there were massive battles in here ... with her, and between her and Ramphele. She left in 1994 when she went on to parliament as a representative of the Inkatha Freedom Party. She's since passed on.

" ... there must be more to this, to what we're doing, than that: how horrible people are to other people ... Which doesn't mean we don't have to work towards exposing a neoliberal enemy"

J: You mentioned last time, this moment that I thought was really interesting. You said you were sitting in the front office with—

M: Martin West ...John Sharp ... probably Emile Boonzaier.

J: —and listening on the radio, De Klerk saying that he was going to release Mandela, and how ... the purpose that anthropology had here was going to have to change after that.

M: It is. And I'm not sure that we've actually found the answer.

Because we still ... get some who push the ... who're always so concerned about—phrases which we used to use—'exposing beastliness'. So much that you kind of think, well, there must be more to this, to what we're doing, than showing how horrible people are to other people.

J: You can study that anywhere.

M: Yeah, so why would anybody want to make that the focus of a discipline? Um, which doesn't mean we don't have to work towards exposing a neoliberal enemy. But it's much more difficult than the apartheid enemy. Because a neoliberal enemy is in amongst us all the time, and all sorts of things about everything we do is that enemy. So it's in ourselves. Um, so that's much more difficult to do battle with ... than the sort of broad ideology which manifests in a political system.

J: And it's interesting that it's a battle metaphor as well, that there's always some enemy we must be fighting.

M: Yeah ... yeah I think every time we have these enemy things, we have to kind of get behind them and say, "What's the positive?" I mean, years ago I remember being in the field, going to Matatiele in the then recently independent Transkei with some students ... to the local magistrate-cum-district administrator. And [I] said, "Look I'm coming here with these bunch of people, and just want to let you know that we'll be here a few weeks; Here we are, and here are our documents. This is who we are, and this is where we'll be", and getting it cleared through the system. And he was a black man, he was not a nice man, and he was very officious ... and we came out of there, and the students were sort of ... hating him. And I said, "why?" [They said,] "Well he was so nasty and he was so" ... this and that. And I said,

Well ... put yourself in his shoes. He's in a frustrating job, he's an intelligent man ... the opportunities which you'll have—we were all white—that you and I have had ... which he was unable to ever have—they weren't there for him. This is what he was able to do. He can't get much higher, because ... he's in the Transkei. There's not much further to go. He could become a chief magistrate or something, but there's nowhere else to go. The world is very small for him. And of course he's going to become like that, and he just does the job in that sort of way. Try and understand him.

And they really struggled. I'm saying that because we do need to kind of look and say, "Well, what are the positives which come out of things?"

I mean the development ... the post-development discourse, which makes development just destructive of everything. Regional development ... brings all sorts of unintended consequences, which are negative. And yes it does, development interventions do that. But also there are some positives which come out, some people seize what's made available—they experience what they've been exposed to as valuable. So ... why don't we write about those as well? We do, of course, get some people who do, like David Mosse who does even as he critiques the development industry at large.

[David Mosse] kind of turns it around a bit. And he's by no means saying, "This is the be-all and end-all of the future and just go down this route and we'll …"—'cause he's really critical of the development exercise. But he's also recognising some of the positives and some of the benefits, again, often unintended. And then he points out, well, part of the problem is that policy, and policy-makers, can't see those as benefits, because the benefits they can see are only what they expected to have arisen as benefits. So, for them, the project has been unsuccessful in their terms, or successful in their terms, but only in terms of their own goals. So Mosse is, kind of then, again, attacking the policy-makers and the development planners, for not being … sensitive enough to recognising when things do go right for the wrong reasons, or for reasons which they didn't anticipate. And there are positive—they have beneficial spin offs. So that's, I suppose, what you need to do; kind of use that way of looking at things.

J: For anthropologists wanting to study development or NGOs, for example, what is there to do in that field without just reiterating the post-development critique?

M: Well one of them is to go beyond the post-development critique to say, "Despite all the negatives, what are the benefits here?" Yeah, positives, that people regard as positive. …What most of that work has failed to do until recently is ask the questions about why the NGOs and their funders … expect what they do and what the consequences are of their having and imposing those expectations.

J: And continue to be a thriving business despite all the critique that's come out, and structural adjustment being a failure, according to everyone.

M: Yeah, that's right. Years ago one of my Honours students did [a sport related NGO study] … Now, before she did that, long before she did that, another student worked with the same NGO, actually … The student that I worked with—the Honours student

86

years before that—was really keen to get into a project where she could do good for people; and she was a sports person and had found this NGO, and met somebody who introduced her to the leaders. And she was all kind of gung-ho about how she was going to go work with them and work in the townships with them and really be good for the kids and stuff. And she went off and she started working with them.

Yet, she reported, she hardly ever was able to leave the NGO's office. Partially because their administrators there, their programme conveners, organisers who were supposed to go off to the field hardly ever went out; partly because the guy who was in charge never gave them the resources to go out and do very much. But he kept on pulling in resources and gave [people] more jobs. And she couldn't see that as a positive. And that's part of the problem of an Honours or even a short Master's, study like you're doing. You don't have time to then go and say, "Well, look at those people and their families" and say ... "Well ... their children are now being educated, and maybe able to get into something better than where they were a generation back; where they would have been had this opportunity not come". It's very slow, long-term, trickle-down .... I don't believe that trickle-down is all we need, we definitely need big-bang change, but ... let's not write off all the trickle-down simply because there hasn't been big-bang change. So those are the kinds of things, And then you've got to rethink, "What does trickle-down really mean? And how does it work?"

***

"Should there be A South African anthropology, or should it be diverse? I think probably the latter, without being so diverse that we can't talk to each other"

J: ... In terms of UCT and this department, maybe compared to other departments, did you feel that there was

kind of a mission statement or ... an idea of what the UCT department ... was on a trajectory of being ... in anthropology in South Africa? With the [recent transition in Humanities departments] ... is there still an idea of what this department might be?

M: Well, I mean there was a—and again I'm not sure it was planned ... Monica Wilson—though there were others around who were sort of well know, like Eileen Krige—Monica stood out. I think, head and shoulders over [Krige] and in some ways over Philip Mayer. I'm not quite sure—yeah, I know why, partly because she was just more of a public intellectual, and published more. And Philip didn't publish a hell of a lot, so he didn't quite make the same name for himself, even though *Townsmen or Tribesmen* was so widely prescribed, especially in the US, through the late '60s and '70s. And he wasn't as well connected internationally. Eileen Krige was much more ethnographically focused than really challenging what anthropology was about. I mean, Monica, despite—it certainly wasn't a great ... in retrospect ... these 'Oxford History of South Africa' [volumes] are not great books, looked at from now, but they were really major texts when they came out and they had an enormous impact ...

J: Do you think there is also something to be said about— and maybe it's changed now—trying to publish a monograph or a book versus getting several articles out each year?

M: Books have a longer lifespan unless the article that you publish is a major seminal piece. I mean, a piece like Harold Wolpe's on cheap labour in 1972, or Colin Bundy's around the same sort of time, were really seminal and widely recognised, and still used. And there are others like Sherry Ortner's 1984 piece on Practice. Those kind of stand out as everybody knows them; but you have to really be lucky, in some ways, and insightful to find something like that which is going to last. Books I think in the end sometimes do last. They have to be good books. There's a lot of real rubbish that gets put on a shelf and never gets looked at again

.... And I think, yeah, Monica did produce quite a lot of stuff. There's also stuff under her first, her maiden name, and I haven't got everything she published. So, yeah there is something in books still … certainly in this discipline.

J: What books stand out to you since the ' 90s?

M: Since the '90s? *The Anti-Politics Machine.* And … *Encounters with Modernity* [both by James Ferguson]. Those stand out. Obviously the Comaroffs' two volume [*Of Revelation and Revolution*], they stand out. Um … others that really stand out? One book that stands out for me that I don't use much, used a long time ago, is a book by Rob Borofsky called *Making History* … uh, on the Pacific Island, called *Pukapuka* [*and Anthropological Constructions of Knowledge*], which remains major and sort of significant in my mind because it showed how tradition is constructed and reconstructed, depending on the circumstances, in a very, sort of, detailed, ethnographic way. Not many people know it, it seems, so maybe it just worked for me. What others stand out? I dunno … I'll have to think about that.

J: Well 'the Keywords', 'the new Keywords' (2008), really stands out for me as well.

M: Does it? The new one? Really? The old *Keywords* did enormously [well], I don't think the new one is anywhere near as … Yeah, and that's 1988, so it doesn't fall into your post-1990 period. I think Fiona's book [*Raw Life, New Hope*]—recent book [from 2010]—is going to remain quite a significant text. But I might be wrong. It's hard to know that in advance.

J: How do you see anthropology in South Africa, compared to the AAA (American Anthropological Association) for example, or anthropology being done elsewhere?

M: Well, it's so different because it's so much smaller, for one. And it's still relatively parochial … despite the kind of visitors who come in, which may mean it becomes a little bit more—it's not as cohesive ... I mean—going to the [recent Anthropology Southern Africa] conference—occasionally there's a really outstanding student from somewhere else, but as a group ... our [UCT] stuff, our student stuff, stands out ahead of [of other South African universities]. There was this one occasion where ... a Pretoria student who stood out, um, [and] there was one a couple of years ago who wrote the piece on—which we used, I think, last year for [our] first-year [course]—on schooling for pregnant girls.

J: Oh, yes. Is that the 'Sick with Child?'

M: *'Sick' with Child* [by Nina Botha in 2010], yes. She also stands out, from Pretoria. Um ... there was the one—who won the prize this last year? Um, I think that was a pretty good paper. He was a Wits student. But they're relatively few and far between. And ... at least some of the students who come here from other [South African] universities and do an Honours or Master's with us, [they] don't prove to be as good as most of ours. Which isn't to say all of ours are very good. We've had some real dodos of our own making. But I think we're doing okay ... but why am I actually saying all this? Oh, how did I think ... what is the role of this department—

J: What does this department want to be as an anthropology department in South Africa, but also South African anthropology as a contribution to the discipline in general?

M: Yeah, that's much more difficult because it isn't coherent. And so it's hard to know what the contribution of South African anthropology might be. Should there be *a* South African anthropology, or should it be diverse? I think probably the latter, without being so diverse that we can't talk to each other.

***

J: Jean and John Comaroff have their new book coming out, I'm not sure when, but the title seems really interesting: 'Theory from the South'. They claim that the knowledge production coming out of the global south is really going to be taking centre stage, they predict, in the future because ... the global north is now having to grapple with things that the global south has been dealing with all along.

M: In a funny way, we could have told them that in 1988 when we published *Keywords,* because *Keywords,* the first *Keywords,* was a fascinating book, I think, because ... it had a deconstructionist analysis without anybody involved really knowing what deconstruction was. And that was because of the context in which we found ourselves. We just had to do it. I had never heard the word 'deconstruction' when I wrote the stuff, the piece, which is in there, which originally appeared in *Critique of Anthropology,* in a slightly different form. It was originally written in a different form and appeared in *Critique* a little bit later. Um ... and sort of taking images and looking at those and how they represented 'traditionality' was not something which we'd done before, and no one else was doing it. Later, then, others came out. There was a book on National Geographic, Lutz and Collins—And that book came out well afterwards; and, I mean, and they're doing the same sort of stuff. In more depth and more thoroughly, looking at one particular journal, and doing a very good job of it. But ... what we were doing was happening—what they were doing, we were doing—without knowing quite what we were doing, because the context made us do it.

... I mean: think, I think some of the stuff that Lesley [Green] is now doing [on political ecology, contested ecologies and indigenous knowledge], that her students are doing, is quite important. I think the environmental stuff is crucial, and the critique of science. But it's not as if it's unique or special here. It's being done all over the world. So I think that ... again I go back to

Fiona Ross's book, it's taking what we used to do and making it move forward in a very interesting way and I think that that, for me, would be the most interesting way to go. And I don't think others are doing that yet.[6]

J: What about the stuff in the last twenty years, the post-colonial critique?

M: But isn't that the same …? It's anthropology, and anthropology is doing that, but surely we've got to get past that now. We've said it. How many more times have we got to say that the colonial environment produced certain outcomes; and its residue, its legacy, remains with us and keeps on reappearing. Um, you can say it, but you know, there must be another step. It's a bit like the post-development analysis, or critique, which sort of said well, "Development is all bad", and I think … Ferguson's *Anti-Politics Machine* points it out in a really good way, and Escobar picks it up from Ferguson, actually, and runs with it in a much more sophisticated way, albeit with much less ethnography. But, you know, it's … we've got to get over that now, which is not to say that we should ignore it; but we've got to find a way to use it and move on, and I think even David Mosse—that's now a six-year-old book—who's sort of saying "We've got to recognise that there are sometimes positive residues of development, even though they weren't what was intended". And the real question is to investigate the policy makers and understand how they try to maintain a fiction of success in terms of their own criteria for assessing success. It's also still quite critical, we've got to go somewhere else.

J: It still seems to me that when someone thinks about doing anthropology or ethnography in Africa … it's considered primarily a place one goes to study development, development-critique or post-colonialism, because that's what

---

6 By 2014 Spiegel added here: Other than, that is, Keith Hart and John Sharp's Human Economy Project at the University of Pretoria which seems to be going in that kind of direction.

Africa is seen as having to offer, as an interesting place to look at those things. Which, then you end up boxing it in ...

M: ...When I ran the conference here in 2006 for The International Union [of Anthropological and Ethnological Sciences], the title was ... something about the post-colony ... 'Transcending the Postcolonial Condition'. What was important about that was what Faye Harrison [an IUAES executive committee member based in Florida] was saying at the time, "Well, this applies as much to us in the States as it does to you guys". So, [*Theory*] *from the South* was being said then— ... "You guys have just had an experience of it, we're experiencing it too and we know about it because we're anthropologists who know what goes on in Africa and Latin America, and we're just [now] seeing it being played out here". Works perfectly, so it's ... yeah ... in that sense I don't think the Comaroffs are saying anything new. They just say it very elegantly.[7]

---

[7] At the time of these interviews, Comaroff and Comaroff's *Theory from the South* had not yet been published, and Spiegel has since pointed out that his comments here were in response to a lecture given at UCT by the authors about the forthcoming book and not the completed work itself.

Chapter 7

What's Left?

"I thought, 'why bother?' Cause the world is—we don't need that stuff, we need to actually know how to sort things out in this place. But here I am doing some of the same"

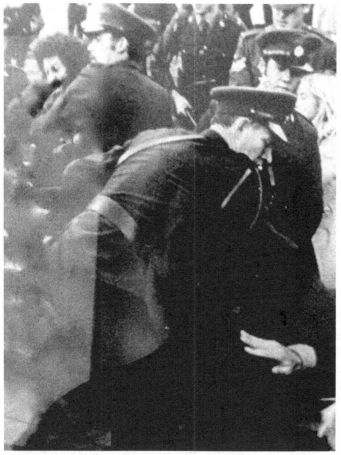

'Reflections': Younger Spiegel photographed in top left corner being grabbed by a police officer – 1973 protest, UCT campus

J: What's left for you in anthropology?

M: Whew. That's a very Francis [Nyamnjoh] question, because I can play with it. Okay, the first was … what is left for me in anthropology? What do I have left to do with anthropology?

J: And what does anthropology have left to do with you?

M: Okay. What do I have left to do with anthropology? Well, I mean the basics are: I have a few more years of teaching to do, and in that teaching I will continue, I hope, to convince people that anthropology is a good way to understand how to be critical of—to be a critical citizen, and to understand the complexities of the world. I hope that I don't stop being an anthropologist at the end of 2014 (when Mugsy is required to retire from UCT). So, I anticipate that what's left—what I'll continue to do—is to use the critical perspective that anthropology has provided me with to continue to develop it, but primarily to use it for arranging different spaces. One would be, I would assume, that the water and sewerage [development research in the townships] that I've been involved in is going to continue.

I hope desperately that I will still be able to do something with the work that I've wanted to do on Rudolph Steiner schools, Waldorf schools. It's something [that] I've sort of promised myself but never got around to doing. I didn't go to one myself. My children went. When I was a child they weren't—the first one started in this country when I was just about to leave primary school and go to high school. Um, there's a fairly strict structure, but it's not the conventional strictness. There's a curriculum, which is said to be linked to the requirements of children as they go through different developmental phases. There's a kind of clear understanding—whether it's the right understanding, I don't know—but it's clear for the teachers that there's a kind of developmental sequence that each child goes through. It's based on Rudolph Steiner's own ideas and it's linked to an idea about reincarnation.

It comes out of theosophy. Steiner was a leading theosophist until he and Madame Blavatsky had a falling-out ... Blavatsky and her crowd decided that they were anticipating the return of the Christ figure, and Steiner said it's not possible. Because he was more of an evolutionist, he said something like, if the Christ figure came there may be another kind of Messianic moment, but it can't be a return, because things are moving onwards. Whether teleological, I'm not sure, but certainly moving onwards. So there was a split between him and the theosophists and ... he then set up what he called anthroposophy. And there's a strong sort of sense in anthropology that each individual comes out of the ether, as it were, out of heaven from the spirit world onto the planet to live a life, which in part is driven by Karma from previous lives. But an individual also has the agency to work with that Karma so that you're not completely determined by Karma or anything like that. You have to interact, so there's a lot of agency in there. And, for example ... a teacher has to work with each child as an individual who comes with their own Karma, with their own prior history, multiple histories which are all merged and submerged, because they don't know them, but they're there. Depending on the child's age, there's a set of, sort of, expected things as they move out of the spirit world and back onto earth.

The Steiner schools work on that principle ... and another part of it is that they try to integrate everything. I'll give you two examples: One is, that when the kids begin to do Newtonian physics, which is at about age twelve or thirteen, somewhere around then ... that sort of point, when they start high school, they teach the industrial revolution. They also teach in big blocks, rather than forty-five minutes for each subject everyday. They start each day with a two-hour block—they call them main lessons—during which they concentrate for three or four weeks on one area or one subject, and one field within that subject, for those weeks for those two-hour blocks. And in the year when they introduce Newtonian physics, they'll start the year, for example, on the history of the industrial revolution, and meanwhile be introducing Newtonian physics and the science behind it; and then they'll have a big block of physics where they'll develop the Newtonian physics and be picking up the industrial revolution stuff alongside. So the kids will understand how physics—how that particular branch of physics—is integrated ... with the historical process.

Another example is ... I've, sort of, sat in on a demonstration class for parents where they showed us what they were doing with geography of our continent. They started off with a topographical map on the wall, and each kid was given an A3 sized piece of board and a piece of chalk, and some clay. And they give you a piece of chalk—or they did with us, anyway—and they said, "Now draw the outline of the continent", and then they said, "Now look at the topographical structures and use the clay to make the ups and downs, the hills and the valleys, mountains and valleys of the continent". And it's amazing what you learn that way.

One of the things we didn't do, but they also do, is they have the kids out on the playground and they hold hands and they form the shape of the perimeter of the continent. Um, and then they shift, so whoever was standing at what would have been the north point of the continent gets shifted to the east or southeast or something, and they each have a chance to be at different points around the continent. So they feel it bodily. And working with the clay in your hands; I mean, the Atlas mountains suddenly are these things which are kind of pulled up here at the top of the, sort of, far end of the board—and the Rift Valley with my right hand I've, sort of, squeezed into the clay .... And it changes your perception of the—It builds it into your bodily sensation—tactile, yeah ... And there's a lot of art and music in it all too.

J: if you did a project with it, do you have a specific angle or question you would try to look at?

M: Well ... I've been very involved in it, cause I'm still on ... the board of a small teacher-training college—offers a Bachelor of Education degree, in Plumstead—the only independent college in the country which has permission, has been accredited, to award a Bachelor of Education degree. And, um, so I'm kind of involved and embroiled in it. But I was very concerned, early on, about the very strong Eurocentric content of what they do, which is linked to

Steiner's ideas of the evolution of consciousness ... not just of mankind, but of consciousness—um, which then ties to particular social epochs; and it's this old evolutionary, sort of, nineteenth century evolutionary stuff. I was concerned about the evolutionism, but also about the Eurocentrism of it, because he didn't draw on any stuff from elsewhere around the world. India a bit, Middle East, India, but that's it. Africa and Latin America just sort of falls out ... it was out of his view and he just didn't know about it.

They introduced [Waldorf Schools] here ... nearly ... fifty years ago. Next year the schools here will be fifty years old. But ... about twenty years ago, I suppose now, they started introducing them to townships ... There's this argument that they should never set up a school without the parents asking for it, but it doesn't always work quite as simply as that. There's meant to be groundswell pressure—demand—for something. But, they set them up in Alexandra and Khayelitsha and in Limpopo province and ... I'm kind of interested to know ... was this fairly Eurocentric curriculum being introduced partly by—funded by—Germans and Dutch funders for black kids? It's been taught in part by volunteers from those countries, from Europe; in part by, it was initially started by whites—South Africans—who were liberal-bent and wanted to do it for black kids. But they are now training black teachers, and I would try and look and see ...to understand ... how do these different categories of people understand what Waldorf education is?

So I've got my ideas, but I want to see how do those volunteers, how do the donors, how do the teacher-trainers and the teachers, and the parents of the children all perceive Waldorf education ... Because in principle the children are not meant to be aware of the underlying principles behind the pedagogical system, they cannot be direct parts of such a study ... that's also part of their development stuff: children under the age of about fourteen are more into their bodies and into their hearts. And the move—the shift—from body to soul, or to heart, comes at the time of permanent teeth falling, the sort of, early teeth, what are they called—milk teeth? And they fall out and the permanent teeth start growing. So there's a kind of seven-year cycle.

J: how has being a teacher, but also a parent maybe, informed your anthropology?

M: Being a parent ... of children who have friends, [and] who themselves, came to this university at a time when there were all sorts of attempts to completely restructure everything in the place. [It] led me into a lot of the administrative stuff that I'm still involved in, because I had to fight the system on behalf of my children's friends. And then others who heard from them that I was fighting to, kind of, enable them to break the system, or to find a way around a very restrictive system ... How that has informed my anthropology? Well, it's taken me into the Waldorf stuff. I would never have gone that way—most of what I've ever written has been political economy type stuff.

That's why, when I came to anthropology, I sat in first-year lectures and I despised all my co-students who were there to learn about the quaint and curious customs and habits—of whoever 'the Bongo Bongo' were—and the ritual and the religion and the magic and stuff, because I thought, well, these are poor people. I'd worked in Lesotho doing voluntary stuff and I wanted to get into the political economy stuff, although I didn't have that word, that phrase, in my head. I knew that those people were struggling, I knew that those people wanted to live, what the ANC now calls, a 'better life'. And I wanted to understand what was it that was undermining that. And so all this kind of wishy-washy, I thought, stuff, which comes up in our course called 'belief and symbolism', was not what I wanted to do. In second-year, I was quite enthralled by the structuralist analysis of kinship and particularly of origin and mortuary myths in Madagascar, but that was because the teacher was very good.

But, it was never—that kind of turned me a bit, but my main interest was always the political, and particularly the economic, and the political as far as it affected the economic. I've hardly written much on that other stuff. Well, the first paper I did which wasn't like that was a paper on extra-marital sex in Lesotho, which was really around myths—or a story about a mythical history—of chiefs and about how that was actually about polygyny. But then it was

100

presented to me as something having to do with extra-marital sex, which was something I bumped into in Lesotho by people simply letting me into a kind of open secret … I, sort of, discovered it in the most interesting way. [I was] sitting in somebody's home, doing my Honours dissertation research. That would have been in '73. Sitting there, in this woman's home … it was a house with multiple houses … a household with—

J: Many doors?

M: Of course, because each house has one door. So it would have counted as more than one household for the idiotic people in this city who count by doors. She lent me one of those houses to stay in; and my assistant and I stayed in there. But we often … [had] supper together. Her husband was away in the mines somewhere and she would often come around and sit and eat together with us, and we'd chat. And one night she had a friend—I think my assistant had gone off to his village—and there I was with these two older women, slightly older than I was. I was … what, mid-twenties. And they were probably in their early thirties. And they said to me, "What's wrong with you?" And I said, "What do you mean what's wrong with me?" "Well, you've been here all these weeks and you haven't found yourself a girlfriend". So I said, "Well, I'm doing this research on migrant labour and its effect on marriage, and I can't really do something like that because that will kind of confound the situation". But I kind of pursued it a bit and I said, "But why do you ask? I mean, surely … you don't kind of just do that sort of stuff?" They said, "No, you're wrong; any other man from Lesotho who came here wouldn't stay for more than a few days without having picked up on one of the women here", and [that included] the married ones whose husbands are away on the mines. Indeed it turned out there was a whole … almost everybody—I mean, I sat down with them and later, at another village, had somebody list every adult woman and whom they had as extra-marital sexual partners, and almost everybody had one or more. And then this one old man told me this happened because of polygyny, because men had many wives, but they didn't necessarily 'service'—to use a

101

horrible term—all those women. And he told this wonderful story, and I've written it, it's published ... in the festschrift for Philip and Iona Mayer—*Tradition and Transition* that Pat McAllister and I edited.

[It was] about how ... I think it was Moshoeshoe, who's now mythologised as a founder of the Basotho. [When he was young, he] had been with another older chief, possibly Monaheng ... he was being taught how to be a good [leader]. And he spent some time with this man in his home, and the old man took him out early one morning, before the sun rose, and they went up on a hill overlooking the village, and the village had a lot of houses, each one of which was the house of a wife of this older man. And, as the sun rose, they saw [each] door open and a man came out of that woman's house, and another man came out of [another] woman's house. And the young man said, "What, but these are your wives! Look at this –"And the older man said, "He's a really powerful warrior, and he'll produce children for me who are warriors. The children are mine because of bride wealth". "And he's a really good councillor, his children will become good councillors. So, I'm building up my lineage". I'm using these as studs, basically! And then this guy [telling me this story] said to me, "And that's why we do it. Because the men are used to being with other men's wives, and the women are used to having other men [to] sleep with. It works out". Except in the time of AIDS, but it wasn't a period of AIDS. This was 1970s that I heard this and AIDS was unheard of in southern Africa at that point.

So, I wrote that up. There was still a little bit of political economy in it, because of the migrant labour and the men being away on the mines; but the myth was most of what it was about, a mythical story. I've written one or two papers like that, the most recent one was a piece out of the Waldorf stuff, it's the only piece I've done [on that]. Part of what I've done as a member of that school board—that teacher-training college board. The people there aren't academics—most of them have been school teachers, and they don't have post-graduate degrees, and the system has required that they have more Master's degree qualifications to be able to teach Bachelor's ... to assess and award Bachelor's degrees. So I supervised a few people …. And one of them was the Eurythmy teacher. Eurythmy's a formal movement discipline …

This was a woman who had a diploma in Eurythmy from a German College. She's a very intelligent woman, and she wanted to get a Master's because she runs the Eurythmy training programme. She did it in the UCT School of Dance with the choreography and stuff that I had nothing to do with; but then the fellow in dance … wasn't willing on his own to supervise the dissertation. And so I worked with her on that very closely. Also she's German-speaking, so I did a lot of, sort of, reworking it to English … Um, so I really got to grips with this stuff. She and I then co-authored a paper on the stuff, which I presented here a couple years ago, um, which doesn't get into the body stuff in the way that Susan Levine and others would have liked me to … I've been critiqued for that. But I wrote a Levi-Straussian analysis … of what they're doing, or it brings a Levi-Straussian analysis into it. When I presented it at a conference in Europe … it was the first time I really kind of moved completely away from anything to do with political economy. There's nothing in the paper like that.

Being a parent has drawn me into that stuff, I suppose, stuff which I would never have gone into, I don't think. I've been really critical of people like Hammond-Tooke who wrote structuralist analysis, of space and stuff, and mythology in South Africa. I thought, "why bother?" Because the world is—we don't need that stuff, we need to actually know how to sort things out in this place. But here I am doing some of the same.

"…just to get a sense of where the discipline is moving and what—because it's your generation that drives it, not us"

M: So there you are, there's how being a parent has done it. So what's left for me of anthropology? I think those kinds of things. The other thing I'd like to do is … I'd like to get to every university in this country and spend enough time there to read all the Master's Dissertations and PhD theses that have been submitted in the last five to ten years and get an overall sense of what's happening to the discipline in this country.

J: At the other universities?

M: Well, I haven't read them all here either. It would be a hell of a lot of reading. And I'd not have to read them from cover to cover. But just to get a sense of where the discipline is moving and what—because it's your generation that drives it, not us ... Um, we've gotta ... you get to a point where you've actually got to let go and let the younger generation take it over. And so I'd like to do that and kind of get an overview and write that up. And, along with that, I'd like to stop at the various places in the country where I've—on the sub-continent—where I've done research and just spend a few days, weeks or more, in each of them, and just see what's changed. Whether I can write that up or not, I don't know.

J: What's anthropology got left to do with you?

M: Well, clearly it's going to use me to continue to do some teaching. I'm still [in 2011] on the association council—the national/regional one. I'm on two international ones too. Um ... the one goes on until 2013 when I'll hopefully be able to get out of it, the other one is a four-year term from last year, so 2014. Um, but it might turn into more, I dunno. ... What more is the discipline going to do with me?

It's hard to know, what does a discipline do with people? It could just spit me out. I dunno, it's hard to know. I'd like some of my work to continue to be useful, to be drawn on by others. I was talking to one of the Honours students, who is heading off to the Eastern Cape just today. It's clear that there's a whole lot of what I've written in the past which our undergraduates and graduates and junior post-graduates need to know in order to do the kind of research [that that student] wants to do, and she doesn't. I'm not the only one. Lesley [Green] will tell you that quite a lot of her stuff derives from stuff that I wrote.

Yeah, a little piece I wrote about—I was asked to act as a consultant on a land restitution claim in KwaZulu-Natal, around Lake St Lucia. Hyoh! ... late '90s, I think. I flew out there twice and wandered around. I was asked to help to determine who had lived there previously. I didn't understand why I needed to do this, because I thought there were surely records of who was dispossessed at the time. But the Land Claims Commissioner there at the time, Cherryl Walker, who's now, or was, head of sociology/anthropology at Stellenbosch; somebody I've known for a long time. [She] felt the need to get some on-the-ground stuff going. There were just two one-week periods. There was no way we could do a full scale archeology of the place, dig-up wherever, look for sites, look for houses and try and work out who was there from that kind of data. The best we could do was walk around the place with people who were clearly from that area and get a sense of who'd been there and who hadn't. And we did that. This was in a game park area, and at one point we were almost run over by a squealing warthog ... two rows of us were walking in parallel lines in an open field—*veld*—and this animal came chasing down, right down between us. And there were hippos and, you know, you couldn't go ... and crocs, and hippos are dangerous things.

Anyway ... So, this was kind of tricky territory to be in. There were these, I don't know, twenty or so of us, a bunch of men who had lived there before, older men, and me, and a surveyor, and someone from the national park, wandering around this place. And these men—it was amazing. Some of [the area] had been turned into plantation, some of it. And the part which had not been, but had become a nature reserve kind of returned to so-called pristine nature. The men walked across these areas and they just ... they knew where the villages and houses had been; and they walked along paths which I couldn't see. And they stopped and they said, "Here is where so-and-so's house was". And we dug around—not dug, just fiddled around—in the bush, and we found stuff that was clear evidence of a house, and the game ranger guy said, "Yes, I know that these bushes only grow where people have lived".

... We found old tin mugs and stuff, and they walked us around this place, along paths, which they could see but I couldn't. And they kept on stopping and saying, "Here and here", and it was an astonishing experience for me, because they knew the paths without being able to see them. And this isn't a place where there—it's on the coast so its got dunes and stuff, but it's not—there's no kind of nice, easy to recognise, topographical features which you can get your bearings from … and they just did it. And then we went to the area where the plantations were, these gum plantations—there they couldn't do anything. All they could do was stand at a path and say, "We can give you a map of how people's homes were situated relative to others, but we can't, we can't"—and we tried, we walked in around the trees, and they couldn't show me anything. I wrote a paper about what I called 'bodily memory' … and how it was destroyed by this plantation. And that stuff, Lesley's picked up on. And, again, that was influenced in part by my Waldorf stuff. So the two came together … In fact, the very first paper I wrote about *that* was a little one—I don't know, probably 250 words—for the school newsletter about that experience, and about how what I'd seen there was something which our children were being taught.

"I know the system here better than most"

M: Okay, so what is anthropology going to do with me still? I don't know …

J: Do you feel like, in 2014, when you're supposed to be done, is it going to let you go? Can you just go?

M: Well, that isn't what they said the other day. I made some comment about it and they said, "No, we're having you back". Yesterday, I was at a meeting, not with anthropologists, actually, to do with the new School [of African and Gender Studies, Anthropology and Linguistics into which Anthropology has been drawn]. I said, "Whenever we do it, you know, in a couple years time I'm going to be gone …" and they said, "No, no, we're going to have you back here as an emeritus, you're going to give us all sorts of advice". And, I guess, I'm not sure if it's anthropology or the university, because I think we need to distinguish between them—because I know the system here better than most.

Not that there aren't others—there are certainly others who know it better than I do—but I know how to manipulate the ... I know how to work it. And I know reasonably well how that works. And ... while I have that skill, I'm sure I'll be turned to. But you lose it quite quickly because it changes so quickly ... I mean, as soon as I stepped down as head of the department, went on sabbatical, and came back ... I remember talking to the dean and I said to her, "There are all sorts of things which—because I'm not on this committee and that committee anymore—I just don't know how it works". And the personnel changes and you just don't know the dynamics anymore. So ... that's a fairly transient knowledge, because the system doesn't remain fixed. It's very people-dependent. Yeah ... so, whether I'll be turned to for any help, who knows. I'm certainly not going to do as Sally [Frankental] has done and go travelling around the world teaching, I don't think, on IHP stuff [The School for International Training's (SIT) 'International Honours Program']. But whether I'm pulled in to do the occasional lecture, or to do some temporary teaching, or ... it depends on what. If the people who remain want me, and it depends on who they are, and it depends on the switch to the new School, if that happens or not, and I ... there's all sorts of stuff, who knows. It's hard to know what I'll be pulled back into, if anything.

" ...Because we're trying to transform ...
...and what does it mean for the institution?"

J: Have you ever thought about doing some kind of 'anthropology of the university'-type project—

M: I have.

J: Do you think that there's value in that?

M: There is, but it's really difficult to do … and I think I would have difficulty. You'd have to do it while you're working here. And then there's the ethical question. It's really difficult to do it completely from the inside … To do something like that, I would want them to do it at a university which wasn't their place, because … somehow there's a little bit of distance. None of it is self-interested. I think if anybody was going to do an anthropology of UCT it should probably be a non-UCT based anthropologist, and probably not a UWC [University of Western Cape] or Stellenbosch-based one either. Preferably, somebody from outside the country [would do it] because there are too many jealousies around the country [and] between universities.

It would be bloody difficult, because people assume that whatever you're doing is looking after your own interests. I mean, one of the things I've always really wanted to do, and I wish I could find a way to do it is … it goes back to years ago when they first said, "We've got to get more black staff on board". And, as I said—this was *years* ago—I was out at some kind of university forum and I said to the then-deputy vice-chancellor, who then became the vice chancellor elsewhere but has since retired … I mean, it's *years* ago. And I said to him, "What you need to realise is that the people you're wanting to attract here have to earn a better salary than what you're paying, because they're first generation—for the most part, that's changing a bit now, but at that point—they're first generation middle class people. And their parents are working class, or even worse off than that. Whatever has enabled them to get where they've got financially, has to be paid back … to the next child in line, or the nephew, or the cousin, or somebody, and the salaries you pay here at UCT don't pay enough". And [the deputy vice-chancellor] couldn't understand.

What I really would like to do … without knowing who the people are … is, go to every member of the academic staff here, or a good sample, and [find] out how many of them are children of parents who've got money, who are supporting them, helping to support them. I mean … I was one. My home was bought with help

108

from my parents. My children's schooling, private schooling, was paid for by my parents. [Who here knows they have] a security from that, or, who are married to somebody else, who's also earning a reasonable amount of money so that there's a cushion for them. I mean, [a] person who comes here [from] that poor, sort of, context who marries someone from a similar background ... I mean, we've seen it over and over again. We see it with Francis [Nyamnjoh], even now, and that's not abject poverty by any means at all. He's helping his wife ... I saw that from people in Lesotho. A fellow who became the vice chancellor at the National University of Lesotho eventually, early on started off as a schoolteacher with eight years of schooling and then a teacher's diploma. Then he taught, then he got a matric, then he taught, then he got a degree, then he taught, and then he got a Master's degree, then he got into the university, then he got a PhD. And once he had his PhD and was reasonably established, he then picked up and did the same for his wife ... he then picked her up and made sure she got a degree.

J: Right. That would be a fascinating study ...

M: And I know. I've inherited money. Now that my father's passed on, I'm comfortable. Those who aren't—who don't have that—have a completely different way of having to look at this place (UCT). Others, such as someone married to a successful businessperson can afford to take off for a time—or to do some unusual research. Similarly, someone who is together with a very successful professional ... Their lifestyle makes a lot possible that is not so for someone attempting to support themselves and a number of dependents on a UCT academic salary. I could illustrate here with examples but it's unfair to pick on individuals. Were I to do that kind of research it would have to be extremely ethically sensitive ...

J: Right, even if you just focused on money, and not personal experience, per se, and traced the different people that had that monetary support, generationally, which flows through—

M: Yes, absolutely!

J: —It would be very interesting to learn about how those who work in academia actually get there. Who's supporting them, and how does that monetary support structure the system?

M: Yes, right, right. Yeah, and yet, to do that—when I've mentioned this to people, sometimes, people are *so* resistant. I remember saying it to [someone I know] reasonably well, someone in a biology department, and … I said, "Surely you've inherited …" and suddenly … they won't talk. People are embarrassed by it. Well, they're embarrassed by the fact that they've been supported by other people, which in itself is telling! We're all supposed to be equal and we're not! We're not! Absolute bullshit. So that, for me, would be a fascinating study.

J: At any university, that would be a really interesting study.

M: Yeah, it would be, but here in particular, because we're trying to transform, and transformation means having to turn to people who don't have that background. And what does it mean for the institution?

***

"And then it was apartheid, which was a kind of structure, but it's there, it's exactly the same structure, in a different form, and a much bigger scale"

J: What's left of anthropology? After anthropology, what's left?

M: Okay, what's left of anthropology? I can play with that one. Um, the one answer is: lots more anthropology. Because anthropology hasn't gone and been disappeared, but what's left of anthropology ... is ... what anthropology's lost ... or a lot of anthropology's lost, because of the post-modern turn, the political economy, to the left. That's what I mean by play with the words. What's *to* the left of anthropology is a whole lot of stuff which anthropology was very engaged in ... in the 1970s, '80s, '90s ... which is there still in Fiona [Ross]'s work.

J: Such as?

M: Well ... to demonstrate—to get into the nitty-gritty of—the consequences of a political economic system, structures, which are undermining people's abilities to live the way they would prefer ... It's exactly what took me to Lesotho, what drove all my work. Then it was apartheid, which was a kind of structure, but it's there, it's exactly the same structure, in a different form, and on a much bigger scale. And we don't do it. I mean, our students don't know what political economy means ... they really don't. And they don't want to ... a historicizing of the political economy of a context, they don't want that stuff.

And that's what's to the left of, and it's what's left for, anthropology: to go back to, in a new way, so it doesn't have to be a simple rehearsal—it would be absurd to kind of revive the old neo-Marxism.

J: Do you think the neoliberal turn has ... do you think maybe that has to do with students not wanting to look at [political economy] anymore?

M: Yeah. And also the experience of living in it, in a neoliberal dominated world of having to fight for yourself, and not really for anybody else. The individualism, the atomisation that goes with that ... yeah, all of that. And I think that's left *for* anthropology ... It's what's left *for* anthropology, but it's also *to the left of* anthropology. And, unfortunately, is *now* to the left of anthropology. It should be left for anthropology to go back, to get into again ...

J: What's to the right of anthropology?

M: Oh, we can go back to the, do more of the kind of—I mean, it's fun stuff, *The Balinese Cock Fight* is really fun … but, so what? I mean that's the problem with my stuff about Waldorf, the Eurythmy. It was fun, I've enjoyed it, I've learnt a lot about it, but it … I mean, the only reason I'm keen on it … I hated it when my kids had to do it at school. I teased the teacher, who's actually a good friend of mine now.[8] Her husband was my one child's class teacher for seven years—Oh, there's another thing: the Waldorf schools take children from grade one to grade seven or eight, same teacher, for seven and a half years. [It] becomes like a parent-relationship. And my daughter who had this man as her teacher for seven years treats him, I mean, [when a] birthday comes, she phones him and he phones her. They kind of, I mean, they're family friends as well now, which … his wife was a Eurythmy teacher—I used to taunt her mercilessly about this stuff. And I've learnt now that it actually has some significance, very great significance, which is about agency. It's about learning to know your space, where you are in the world, but you'll have to read our paper about some of that stuff.

"And I want to know what's the next way of drawing the map. Is there a different—or whatever it is—picture?"

M: Um, what was your other question?

J: After anthropology, what's left?

M: Um, it's not after anthropology—it's the same question as the previous one. Um … well I mean, more anthropology, and again what's left, what is to the left, is the anthropology we ought to be doing.

---

[8] She has since passed away.

J: You could also take the question more personally as well, if anthropology does let you go, for the most part, if it doesn't pull you back—

M: Oh, what's left for me? Institutionally, I may not do anthropology, but I can't imagine—maybe I'm wrong—that the perspectives that I've learned from being an anthropologist, and that I've applied, for the most part, in my life, are suddenly going to disappear because I'm no longer attached to an institution that treats me as an anthropologist. I can't see how that's going to go. I expect I will die an anthropologist. Whatever that means.

Um, I can't see how that's going to suddenly disappear from my life, even if I become a full-time vegetable gardener in my backyard. I won't become a full-time vegetable gardener, because I'll constantly be engaging with other people. I won't sit in my house or room—unless I'm too sick to move—I'm too gregarious a person to be left completely on my own ... So I can't imagine that, because it's not just anthropology, it's also the whole critical perspective—which is where I started, actually—the critical perspective, which comes from anthropology.

Which wasn't, I mean, how I learned it first—there's no way I would teach my students what I was taught ... in the way I was taught it, as a new undergrad anthropology student. I would never stand up and sort of give the details of the Pondo marriage system, or the Pondo kinship system or anything like that in the sorts of ways it was taught to me. I might say I want you to read about it, I would want you to understand the principles behind it, but I wouldn't teach it the way I was taught it. But, in the process of learning that stuff, I learnt the value of comparison, and the value of comparison for critical understanding of self and [one's] own way of doing things. That I'm not going to lose or abandon.

J: How do you answer people today when they ask you, 'what is anthropology?'

M: Oh. Well, if I'm asked at open-day, for example, I say, "How long do you wanna talk?" Briefly, the comparative study of human society and culture through time and space. For me … it's not so much what it is, but what it provides: that critical perspective from comparative analysis. Being able to look at what I do, what people around me do, in ways which say this isn't normal, isn't necessarily normal, isn't necessarily right … other people do it differently. Now, let's look at their way of doing things and compare those with ours and say "Well, why are we doing what we're doing the way we are? There's a logic behind it, but what is the logic?" And if we unpack the logic, we'll see whether the logic is, whether the rationale has a … uh, is based on false premises or not.

That will continue. And that, for me, ultimately, is what the discipline is for. For most, I mean, very few people become anthropologists and practise anthropology, except in life. How many people in the world—you know, there are hundreds of thousands who do undergraduate courses in anthropology and even get majors and first degrees in anthropology, but they don't become professional anthropologists. And a guy like Charles Carter, who's an executive director now of AngloGold Ashanti, he did an undergraduate and Honours with us. [He] went to Oxford, got a PPE PhD there, because the anthropology that was offered there at the time was so 'Bongo Bongo'—alterity stuff—and [he] uses his anthropology all the time as an executive director of a big mining company.

Many of our students will tell us that; ex-students will tell us that. " …If it hadn't been for anthropology, I wouldn't have done what I'm doing, I wouldn't have known how to address what I'm having to do". And it's really that critical perspective. Now, you can probably get it elsewhere. Philosophy certainly tries to develop it. I'm not convinced sociology does—sometimes, and sometimes not. History has the potential to, but it ends up being more history and not enough historiography … anthropology isn't only ethnography. That's what's interesting about it. It's history, it's ethnography with an analysis and a developing set of theoretical perspectives that it simultaneously builds and reflects on.

J: The difference seems to be the kind of work that it tries to put the information it gathers to. Not necessarily just practical ways, like policy-making, but also with theory ... the kind of moulding it tries to do.

M: Right. What work does this information and this material that you've gathered, what work can it do? That's right, and these stories, for the most part, pick up on some ideas and they seem simply to use them to produce a narrative of what happened. Years ago, Shula Marks, a leading southern African historian who was based at that point in London ... came here [to UCT and] presented a paper. She was one of the southern African social historians building on the work of E.P. Thompson. She ... developed that older Marxist stuff, sort of ... the neo-Marxist stuff—split between structuralist-Marxists and the social historians—amongst these historians. And she was one of the leaders of the social history movement.

I remember she presented a paper, which was fascinating, but ... one of the things she was saying was that you've got this way of understanding things now, and we need now to have people work all over the sub-continent, giving the details about various pasts to fill in the picture. We've got an overall picture, but we need to know the details of each particular perspective, each particular region, because it's never the same—which I agree with completely. Yet, I asked, "But, Shula, what's the next step? Intellectually, what's the next"—and she didn't like the question. Because I was saying, "We've got to this point in your theorising about how to understand the world, and now all you're wanting to do is—you've got the model laid out ... or the map, the picture—and you want everybody else to colour in their little corner in the appropriate way. And I want to know what's the next way of drawing the map. Is there a different—or whatever it is—picture?" She didn't like it. And I think we've done that ... [anthropology] has shifted from that and continues to do so. That was the political economy stuff, and we're constantly shifting. ... There you go. Does that help?

Spiegel in his UCT office, Arts Block 2014, looking at photo negatives from his Lesotho field research

Photographs from field work in Lesotho, 1976/7

Chapter 8

Coda

J: What do you hope anthropology remembers you for?

M: Shyoh! Shyoh. ...It is a nice [question], but it's a really difficult one to answer ... Anthropology, or anthropologists in the future? Well, I'm not sure that they will remember me ... I'll go down in some kind of record. If you were to have asked me this thirty years ago, I would've told you for work on Lesotho, and for a particular perspective on it ... but, that disappeared: the development stuff, the migrant labour stuff, and the political economy analysis, the economic analysis. And that's still there as part of that—as my history and it doesn't go away, but it's not a kind of dominant theme in my thinking [anymore].

I suppose it would be ... I would *like* to be ... thought of as somebody who had the capacity to be flexible, to think flexibly, to think outside the box, at least sometimes. Um, to challenge, sort of, prevailing ideas, although these days I'm probably the one who prevails with them rather than challenges, I'm not sure. I know that students from other campuses come to the annual ASnA conference each year terrified of me—with advance warning—for some other reason, because I ask challenging questions, I guess. And I'm not averse to that being part of my memory.

I can't say that there's a particular analytical theme or analytical thread ... It's much more eclectic and ... and it's shifted. What I do has shifted ground quite a lot. The one thing, which did remain central for quite a long time, was concern over kinship, kin relationships, in various ways. But even that has kind of ... dissipated at this point. So ... yeah, I suppose it's the ability to think around various ideas ... and to challenge ... um ... I guess. I would also like to imagine that ... that my role in this department would be remembered for having first actually kept it alive, because it could easily have died. There was a moment when it was severely under threat—but I not only sought to keep it alive, I believe I actually managed to turn it around into a department—of course with everybody else within it's help! I mean, [I] couldn't have done it on my own. [We turned it] into a department [that] has as many graduate students as it does. I think—and I'm not sure if this is accurate, but I think—at this point this department has more PhDs per member of academic staff than any other in the [humanities] faculty. There are some other departments who've got more, but they've got bigger departments, or more Master's students, but they don't have many PhDs. [The] Psychology [Department] churns them out, particularly at the Master's level. Um ... but ... I think I can claim something, as having done something there.

Quite how I did it, I don't know. Other than being tenacious and defending. There was never a plan other than to maintain and strengthen. It was never kind of strategy—I'm not a chess player—I'm not actually a very good politician, including UCT politics. No, I'm not very good at that stuff. And I'm not a particularly ... occasionally I have Machiavellian thoughts and ideas, but I'm not very good at kind of working out strategising and the tactics from getting from and to a certain point, for getting from A to B. Sometimes tactics, but long term strategy, [I'm] not very good [at], because I do things as I do them. That's part of flexibility, I suppose, it's that the context changes and everything, and I can't actually just hang on to what I thought I had to do. So I shift. So it doesn't make for good long-term strategy.

And, yeah, I do take it as it comes—not with everything. My wife will tell you that I don't, but then that's family stuff ... I mean, obviously there are certain things [that] are, as a head of the department, you can't just let go, because then things fall apart. So there [are] some things [that] come at you in your work and you've got to take them and fight them, but for the most part it hasn't been a planned process. If it had been ... then someone else would have been head of the department long ago. Because that was what I imagined for a long time—that I'd find a successor long ago.

The one thing that I did work at consistently for some years was to get Francis [Nyamnjoh] here. I met him in '98, and I knew from the moment I met him that we had to get him here; and I wasn't yet head of the department. And I've chased him—first managed to get

120

him here as an external examiner; also had him here as a visitor, soon after I first met him. And, [I] just kind of kept at it, on at him, when he was teaching in Botswana, especially. I was in Jo'burg and I took my parents' car, and then they decided that they wanted to come along. We got into the car and we drove up to Botswana for a day, so I could see him and try to convince him.

So ... I suppose, inside the department, in the university ... that's what I'd like to be thought about. And in anthropology generally—in South Africa? I can't imagine. Well, I've also been involved with the various associations, and that sort of stuff, so I guess that will also leave a bit of a mark, but ... with that stuff you can't actually have a major effect. The one thing, as I've said already, that I'd like to do still is to ... look at what anthropologists in this country are really doing. To go from campus to campus and look at dissertations over the last ten years, [see] what they're about. To see whether there are any neat patterns in it and which way it's going and what's influencing people, and whether there really are ... certain influences. And, for a while, this department, when Martin West was the head of the department—and it was his department although John Sharp took over for a while—this department led the pack completely. What we did, everybody else followed, after a while. First they resisted and then they followed. I'm not sure that that is [still] the case. That was also easy then, because it was a country that ... we were isolated so ... the influences from outside were not anywhere near as strong as they are now. And now people have visitors from all over the world and go and visit all over the world, so there are all sorts of other influences.

So ... I supposed that would be what I imagine ... but who knows; who knows whether I'll be remembered that way or not. I may just be forgotten, which is also okay. I'm not so conceited that I think that I need to have my name carved in stone all over the place. Though, in the car yesterday, it was actually quite funny. Yesterday I took Colleen and Marcel [the department office staff] down to Mowbray as I was going with Jonathan to start [toward] the townships and somehow ... we talked about ashes ... after somebody has died. I don't know what [led the conversation]. It may have had something to do with a student [who's] had to go and

121

bury their ancestors, their parents' ashes, or something like that, I've forgotten what it was. And I said something about "Well, maybe they should start creating little cavities in the walls of the Arts Block so people's ashes can be put there". And Marcel said, "Yeah, we can have a memorial to you here like that", and I said, "Well, maybe my ashes should go in there".

J: Part of the wall. Do you feel tied enough to the building?

M: Ah yes! That was what it was, it was because Marcel was saying that I've been there so long I'm just sort of—I said, "I'm no longer just part of the woodwork, I'm actually part of the brickwork". This is how it came up. And then I said, "Maybe when I'm dead my ashes should be put into a slot in the wall of the Arts building". And she said, "Have you been in the Arts building ever since you've been here?" And I said, "Absolutely". As a student, this is where the anthropology department was. This office was my office when I was a tutor. It was a shared office. And this was the tutors' office. That office was, uh—that room that you guys have got next door [the 'post-grad room']—was the tearoom and where we had our most intense departmental seminars ...

Spiegel and Dickson

Bibliography

Abu-Lughod, Lila. 1991. 'Writing Against Culture' in R.G. Fox (ed) *Recapturing Anthropology: Working in the Present*, School of American Research Press, pp. 137-162.

Adesina, J. 2008. 'Archie Mafeje and the Pursuit of Endogeny: Against Alterity and Extroversion', *African Development*, Vol. 33 (4): pp. 133-152.

Appadurai, Arjun. 1990. "Disjuncture and Difference in the Global Cultural Economy." *Public Culture Spring* 2(2): 1-24.

Asad, Talal (ed). 1973. *Anthropology and the Colonial Encounter.* London: Ithaca Press.

Aseka, E. M. and G.R. Murunga. 1997. 'Some Comments on the Mafeje-Moore Debate' *CODESRIA Bulletin,* No.3: pp. 11-14.

Bank, Andrew and Lesley J. Bank (eds). 2013. *Inside African Anthropology: Monica Wilson and Her Interpreters.* London: Cambridge University Press.

Bank, Andrew. 2013. 'Introduction'. In Bank, Andrew and Lesley J. Bank (eds). *Inside African Anthropology: Monica Wilson and Her Interpreters.* London: Cambridge University Press.

Bogopa, D.L. and T.S. Petrus. 2007. 'The Politics of Teaching, Funding and Publication in South African Anthropology: "Our Experiences"'. *The African Anthropologist*, Vol. 14(1&2) pp. 1-18 published by CODESRIA.

Boonzaier, Emile and John Sharp (eds). 1988. *South African Keywords: The uses and abuses of political concepts.* Cape Town and Johannesburg: David Philip.

Coertze, P.J., F.J. Language, and B.I.C. van Eeden. 1943. 'Die Oplossing van die Naturellevraagstuk in Suid-Akrika. Johannesburg.

Clifford, James and Marcus, G. (eds). 1986. *Writing Culture: The Poetics and Politics of Ethnography*, Berkeley and Los Angelos: University of California Press.

CODESRIA Bulletin, No. 3 & 4, 2008 (Special Issue of debates and tributes dedicated to the late Archie Mafeje).

Comaroff, Jean and John L. Comaroff. 1991. *Of Revelation and Revolution: Christianity, Colonialism and Consciousness in South Africa.* Chicago: University of Chicago Press.

—1992. *Ethnography and the Historical Imagination.* Boulder: Westview Press.

—1999. 'Occult Economies and the Violence of Abstraction: Notes from the South African Postcolony.' *American Ethnologist,* Vol. 26, No. 2 (May), pp. 279-303.

— 2004. 'Criminal obsessions, after Foucault: Postcoloniality, policing, and the metaphysics of disorder'. *Critical Inquiry*, 30(4), 800-824.

— (eds.) 2008. *Law and Disorder in the Postcolony.* University of Chicago Press.

— 2009. *Ethnicity, Inc.* University of KwaZulu-Natal Press.

— 2012. *Theory From the South: Or, How Euro-America is Evolving Toward Africa* Boulder and London: Paradigm Publishers.

Devisch, Rene and Francis B. Nyamnjoh (eds). 2011. *The Postcolonial Turn: Re-Imagining Anthropology and Africa.* Cameroon: Langaa Research and Publishing Common Initiative Group.

Ferguson, James. 2006. *Global Shadows: Africa in the Neoliberal World Order.* Durham and London: Duke University Press.

Geschiere, Peter. 2009. *The Perils of Belonging: Autochthony, Citizenship, and Exclusion in Africa and Europe.* Chicago: University of Chicago Press.

Gluckman, Max. 1940. 'Analysis of a Social Situation in Modern Zululand'. *Bantu Studies*, Vol. 14(1) pp. 1-30.

Gordon, Robert J. 1988. 'Apartheid's anthropologists: the genealogy of Afrikaner anthropology'. *American Ethnologist,* 15(3) pp. 535-553.

Gordon, Robert. J. and Andrew D. Spiegel. 1993. 'Southern Africa Revisited.' *Annual Review of Anthropology,* 22 pp. 83-105.

Gupta, Akhil. and James Ferguson. 1992. 'Beyond "culture": Space, identity, and the politics of difference'. *Cultural anthropology,* 7(1), 6-23.

—1997. 'Discipline and Practice: "The Field" as Site, Method, and Location in Anthropology' in Akhil Gupta and James Ferguson (eds), *Anthropological Locations: Boundaries and Grounds of a Field Science. Berkeley:* University of California Press.

Hammond-Tooke, W. D. 1962. *Bhaca Society.* Cape Town: Oxford University Press.

—1997. *Imperfect Interpreters: South Africa's Anthropologists 1920-1990.* Johannesburg: Witwatersrand University Press.

Harvey, David. 2005. *A Brief History of Neoliberalism.* Oxford and New York: Oxford University Press.

Henderson, Patricia. 2011. *AIDS, Intimacy and Care in Rural KwaZulu-Natal: A Kinship of Bones*. Amsterdam: Amsterdam University Press.

Hunter (Wilson), Monica. 1936. *Reaction to Conquest: Effects of Contact with Europeans on the Pondo of South Africa*. London: Oxford University Press.

Hutchinson, Sharon. 1996. *Nuer Dilemmas: Coping with Money, War, and the State*. Berkeley, Los Angeles, London: University of California Press.

Keesing, Roger. 1994. 'Theories of culture revisited' in *Assessing Cultural Anthropology* R.Borofsky (ed). New York: McGraw Hill pp.301-310.

Krige, Eileen J. 1936. *The Social System of the Zulus*. Pietermaritzburg: Shuter and Shooter.

Krige, Eileen and Jack Krige. 1943. *The Realm of a Rain-Queen: A Study of the Pattern of Lovedu Society*. London: Oxford University Press.

Kuper, Adam. 1995. Reply to Scheper-Hughes, Nancy. 'The Primacy of the Ethical: Propositions for a Military Anthropology'. *Current Anthropology*, Vol. 36(3) pp. 409-440.

—1998. 'Anthropology in South Africa: An Inside Job.' *Working Papers in African Studies No. 212. Boston University.*

Levine, Susan. 2013. *Children of a Bitter Harvest: Child Labour in the Cape Winelands*. South Africa: HSRC Press.

Lodge, Tom. 1985. 'White Power and the Liberal Conscience: Racial Segregation and South African Liberalism, 1921-60'. *Journal of Southern African Studies*, 11(2) pp. 337-339.

Low, Setha and Sally Engle Merry. 2010. 'Engaged Anthropology: Diversity and Dilemmas'.*Current Anthropology*, vol. 51(S2): pp S203-S226. Published by The University of Chicago Press on behalf of Wenner-Gren Foundation for Anthropological Research.

Macfarlane, David. 2011. 'UCT in war over "bantu education"'. *The Mail&Guardian*. Published March 11th.

Mafeje, Archie. 1981. 'On the Articulation of Modes of Production: Review Article.' *Journal of Southern African Studies*, 8(1) pp. 123-138.

— 1991. *The Theory and Ethnography of African Social Formations: The Case of Interlacustrine Kingdoms*. London: CODESRIA.

— 1998. 'Anthropology and Independent Africans: Suicide or End of an Era?' *African Sociological Review*, Vol.2(1):1-43.

— 2000. 'Africanity: A Combative Ontology', *CODESRIA Bulletin*, No. 1 pp. 66-71.

Malkki, Liisa. 1995. *Purity and Exile: Violence, Memory, and National Cosmology Among Hutu Refugees in Tanzania*. London and Chicago, IL: University of Chicago Press.

Mayer, Philip. 1951. *The Lineage Principle in Gusii Society*. London: Oxford University Press.

—1980. (ed.) *Black Villagers in an Industrial Society: Anthropological Perspectives on Labour Migration in South Africa*. Cape Town and Oxford: Oxford University Press.

Mayer, Philip and Iona Mayer. 1974. *Townsmen or Tribesmen*. Cape Town: Oxford University.

Mbembe, Achille. 2002. 'African Modes of Self-Writing'. *Public Culture*, Vol. 14(1): pp. 239-273 and Duke University Press.

—2008. 'Passages to Freedom: The Politics of Racial Reconciliation in South Africa'. *Public Culture* Vol. 20(1) pp 5-18.

—2011. 'Fanon's nightmare, our reality'. *The Mail&Guardian*. Published December 23rd. http://mg.co.za/article/2011-12-23-fanons-nightmare-our-reality

— 2012. 'Rule of property versus rule of the poor?' *The Mail&Guardian*. Published June 15th. http://mg.co.za/article/2012-06-15-rule-of-property-versus-rule-of-the-poor

—2013. 'Consumed by our lust for lost segregation'. *The Mail&Guardian*. Published March 28th. http://mg.co.za/article/2013-03-28-00-consumed-by-our-lust-for-lost-segregation

Mudimbe, V. Y. 1988. *The Invention of Africa: Gnosis, Philosophy and the Order of Knowledge*. Bloomington and Indianapolis: Indiana University Press.

McAllister, Patrick A. 1986. 'The Impact of Relocation on Social Relationships in a "Betterment" Area in Transkei'. *Development Southern Africa* 3(3).

Murray, Colin. 1981. *Families Divided: The Impact of Migrant Labour in Lesotho*. Johannesburg: Ravan.

— 1983. 'Struggle from the margins: rural slums in the Orange Free State'. In Cooper, Frederick (ed). *Struggle for the City: Migrant Labor, Capital and the State in Urban Africa* pp. 275-318. London: Sage.

— 1987. 'Class, gender and the household: the development cycle in southern Africa'. *Development and Change* 18(2) pp. 235-250.

Murray-Pepper, Megan. 2013. Colin Murray Obituary. The Guardian, Sunday 22 December. http://www.theguardian.com/science/2013/dec/22/colin-murray-obituary

Niehaus, Isak. 1988. 'Domestic dynamics and wage labour: a case study among urban residents in Qwaqwa'. *African Studies* vol. 47(2): pp. 121-144.

Nkwi, Paul Nchoji. 2007. 'Resurgence of Anthropology at African Universities'. *The African Anthropologist*, Vol. 14(1&2) pp. v-vii Published by CODESRIA.

Ntarangwi, Mwenda. 2010. *Reversed Gaze: An African Ethnography of American Anthropology.* University of Illinois Press.

Ntsebeza, Lungisile. 2008. 'The Majefe and UCT Saga: An Unfinished Business?' in *CODESRIA Bulletin*, No. 3 & 4 (Special Issue of debates and tributes dedicated to the late Archie Mafeje) pp. 36-42.

Nyamnjoh, Francis. 2006. *Insiders and Outsiders: Citizenship and Xenophobia in Contemporary Southern Africa.* London and New York: Zed Books.

—2012a. '"Potted Plants in Greenhouses": A Critical Reflection of the Resilience of Colonial Education in Africa'. *Journal of Asian and African Studies,* 47, 2, pp. 129-154.

—2012b. 'Blinded by Sight: Diving the Future of Anthropology in Africa'. *African Spectrum,* 47, 2-3, pp. 63-92.

—2013. 'From Quibbles to Substance: A Response to Responses'. *Africa Spectrum,* 48, 2, pp. 127-139.

Olukoshi, Adebayo and Francis Nyamnjoh. 2008. 'Editorial: A Giant Has Moved On' in *CODESRIA Bulletin*, No. 3 & 4 (Special Issue of debates and tributes dedicated to the late Archie Mafeje) pp. 1-4.

— 2011. 'The Postcolonial Turn: An Introduction' in Devisch, Rene and Francis B. Nyamnjoh (eds). *The Postcolonial Turn: Re-Imagining Anthropology and Africa*. Cameroon: Langaa Research and Publishing Common Initiative Group.

Ortner, Sherry. 1984. 'Theory in Anthropology since the Sixties'. *Comparative Studies in Society and History,* Vol. 26(1) January pp. 126-166 published by Cambridge University Press.

Posel, Deborah. 2001. 'Race as Common Sense: Racial Classification in Twentieth-Century South Africa'. *African Studies Review,* Vol. 44, No. 2, Ways of Seeing: Beyond the New Nativism, pp. 87-113.

Reynolds, Pamela. 1986. *Growing Up in a Divided Society: The Contexts of Childhood in South Africa.* (Edited with Sandra Burman). Johannesburg: Ravan Press.

—1989. *Childhood in Crossroads: Cognition and Society in South Africa.* Cape Town: Philip.

— 2013. *War in Worcester: Youth and the Apartheid State.* New York: Fordham University Press.

Rich, Paul B. 1984. *White Power and the Liberal Conscience: Racial Segregation and South African Liberalism, 1921-1960.* Manchester and Dover: Manchester University Press.

Robins, Steven and Nancy Scheper-Hughes. 1996. 'On the Call for a Militant Anthropology:
The Complexity of "Doing the Right Thing"'. *Current Anthropology,* Vol. 37(2) April pp. 341-346.

Ross, Fiona. 2010. *Raw Life, New Hope: Decency, Housing and Everyday Life in a Post-Apartheid Community*. Claremont: UCT Press.

Said, Edward. 1978. *Orientalism*. New York: Pantheon Books.

Saunders, Christopher. 1988. *The Making of the South African Past, Major Historians in Race and Class*. Cape Town: David Philip.

Scheper-Hughes, Nancy. 1995. 'The Primacy of the Ethical: Propositions for a Military Anthropology'. *Current Anthropology*, Vol. 36(3) pp. 409-440.

—1996. 'Reply' to Robins, Steven. 'On the Call for a Militant Anthropology: The Complexity of "Doing the Right Thing"'. *Current Anthropology*, Vol. 37(2) April pp. 341-346.

Schumaker, Lyn. 2008. 'Women in the Field in the Twentieth Century: Revolution, Involution, Devolution?'. In Kuklick, Henrika (ed.) *A New History of Anthropology*. Oxford: Blackwell Publishing.

Sharp, John. 1980. 'Can we study ethnicity? A critique of fields of study in South African anthropology. *Social Dynamics* Vol. 6 (1):1-16.

—1981. 'The Roots and Development of Volkekunde in South Africa'. *Journal of Southern African Studies*, Vol. 8, No. 1, Special Issue on Anthropology and History (Oct., 1981), pp. 16-36.

—1985. 'Unit of study, context and culture: towards an historical anthropology'. *African Studies*, vol 44(1): pp. 65-86.

— 2008. 'Mafeje and Langa: The Start of an Intellectual's Journey' in *CODESRIA Bulletin*, No. 3 & 4 (Special Issue of debates and tributes dedicated to the late Archie Mafeje) pp. 30-35.

Sharp, John and Andrew Spiegel. 1985. 'Vulnerability to impoverishment in South African rural areas: the erosion of kinship and neighborhood as social resources'. *Africa* vol 55(2): pp. 133-152.

— 1987. 'Relocation, labour migration and the domestic predicament: QwaQwa in the 1980s'. In Eades, Jeremy (ed). *Migrants, Workers, and the Social Order.* London: Tavistock.

Shepherd, Nick and Steven Robins (eds). 2008. *New South African Keywords.* Johannesburg and Athens: Jacana and Ohio University Press.

Sichone, Owen. 2008. 'Xenophobia and Xenophilia in South Africa: African Migrants in Cape Town'. In Werbner, Pnina (ed.). *Anthropology and the New* Cosmopolitanism: *Rooted, Feminist and Vernacular Perspectives,* Oxford: Berg Publishers, pp. 309-332.

Spiegel, Andrew D. 1980. 'Rural differentiation and the diffusion of migrant labour remittances in Lesotho'. In Mayer, Philip (ed.) *Black Villagers in an Industrial Society: Anthropological Perspectives on Labour Migration in South Africa.* Cape Town and Oxford: Oxford University Press.

—1986. 'Fluidity of household composition'. *African Studies* 45(1) pp. 17-36.

—1989. 'Towards an understanding of tradition: uses of tradition(al) in Apartheid South Africa'. *Critical Anthropology* vol. 9(1): pp 49-74.

— 1997. 'Struggling with tradition in South Africa: the multivocality of images of the past'. In Bond, George C. and Angela Gilliam (eds). *Social Construction of the Past: Representation as Power.* London and New York: Routledge.

— 2005. 'From exposé to care: preliminary thoughts about shifting the ethical concerns of South African Social Anthropology'. *Anthropology Southern Africa* 28(3/4) pp. 133-141.

— 2007. 'Reproducing criticality: South African social-cultural anthropology's contemporary challenge – the UCT experience'. *Anthropology Southern Africa* 30(3/4) pp. 119-128.

Spiegel, Andrew D. and Patrick A. McAllister. 1991. *Tradition and Transition in Southern Africa.* Johannesburg: Witwatersrand University Press.

Spiegel, Andrew D. and Neil Armitage, Roxanne Beauclair and Nangolo Ashipala. 2010. 'Draining the shantytowns: Lessons from Kosovo informal settlement, Cape Town, South Africa. In J.-L. Bertrand Krajewski and B. Chocat (eds). GRAIE – Groupe de Recherche Rhne-Aples sur les Infrastructures et lÉau. ISBN 978-2-917199-01-5.

Spiegel, Andrew D. and Neil Armitage, Kevin Winter and Elizabeth Kruger. 2008. 'Community-focused greywater management in two informal settlements in South Africa. *Water Science and Technology* 59(12): pp. 2341-2350.

Thornton, Robert. 1988. 'The quest for community'. In Boonzaier, Emile and John Sharp (eds). *South African Keywords: The uses and abuses of political concepts.* Cape Town and Johannesburg: David Philip.

Webster, David. 1988. 'Class and rural differentiation in a rural Kwa-Zulu community'. Presented at the Association of Anthropology Southern African at Rhodes University.

West, Martin. 1979. *Social anthropology in a divided society.* Inaugural lecture. University of Cape Town.

— 1988. 'Confusing categories: population groups, national states and citizenship' in Emile Boonzaier and John Sharp (eds). *South African Keywords*. Cape Town: Philip.

Whisson, Michael. 1986. 'Advocates, brokers and collaborators: anthropologists in the real world'. In Grillo, Ralph and Alan Rew (eds). *Social Anthropology and Development Policy*. London: Tavistock.

Wilson, Godfrey and Monica Wilson. 1945. *The Analysis of Social Change: Based on Observations in Central Africa*. Cambridge University Press.

Wilson, Monica.1959. *Communal Rituals of the Nyakyusa*. London: Oxford University Press.

Wilson, Monica and Archie Mafeje. 1963. *Langa: A Study of Social Groups in an African Township*. Cape Town: Oxford University Press.

Wolpe, Harold. 1972. 'Capitalism and cheap labour-power in South Africa: From segregation to apartheid'. *Economy and Society*, 1(4) pp. 425-456.

All interviews with Andrew 'Mugsy' Spiegel were conducted between April and June of 2011, with unrecorded follow-up conversations in January and June of 2014.